I MET

GOD

LAST NIGHT

Jesus didn't call us to religion. He called us to a relationship with Him.

I SAW

GOD

LAST NIGHT

Whoever Said He's Dead, Flat Out Lied!

JENNIFER BAGNASCHI

I Saw God Last Night
Copyright © 2014 by Jennifer Bagnaschi
ISBN-13: 978-0692216255 (Rex Regum)
ISBN-10: 0692216251

Visit the author's website at:
www.JenniferBagnaschi.com

To contact the author, please write to:
J. Bagnaschi
P.O. Box 923
Middletown, CT 06457

Partial editing by marketing writer/editor, Jesse Drake

Interior illustrations © 2014 by Lorenzo D. Jones, Jr.
www.LorenzoComics.com

Some names have been changed in this book to protect the privacy of the individuals.

For my husband, the love of my life, Eddie,

My beautiful and hilarious daughters, Eva and Jewel,

My lovely niece, Harmony,

And my Aussie nephews, Ethan and Cameron.

TABLE OF CONTENTS

Preface

EVER SINCE I WAS a little girl, people would always come up to me and randomly say things like, "You're called" or "God has chosen you." When I was 10 or 11 years old, one lady pastor even said to me, "Jenny, the Bible says that many are called but few are chosen, and you are one of the chosen."

Chosen for *what*? I was never quite sure, up until recently.

During my early teens, God began introducing me to the spiritual realm of Heaven and also the diabolical, although I did see them both manifested in my earlier years. But as I grew older, I experienced so much of the supernatural without understanding why it was happening to *me,* nor did I know what I was supposed to do with my knowledge of it. I would ask God for direction but His answer would always be, "Wait."

In my twenties, I developed a friendship with a young woman from church who had almost the same type of experiences with the divine supernatural as I had. We talked for hours about God and the unmatchable ways of which He does things and how He reveals them to us. This friendship was a relief because I thought I was the only one on planet Earth who experienced these things.

As the years went on, fearless and bold, I began to share my testimony of my supernatural visions and divine encounters. I'd strike up conversations with random people and didn't care who they were. I noticed that when I shared my experiences, eight times out of ten, they would feel something "strange" (their words) happening inside of their body (which is the presence of the Holy Spirit), or they'd tell me they had a similar experience such as my own. The presence of the Holy Spirit part didn't surprise me. The part that did surprise me, however, was that people would mention they had experienced the spiritual realm as I had.

After years of research, I concluded that I *definitely* wasn't the only one who the Lord was using like this; it was happening all over the world! Thousands upon thousands of people from different backgrounds and cultures were having literal visions, visitations and dreams of Jesus Christ and converting to Christianity, regardless of the cost or scrutiny. After realizing my friend and I weren't the only ones experiencing divine encounters with the supernatural realm, my interest in other people's encounters was piqued.

It looked as if Acts 2:17 was coming to pass:

"And it shall come to pass in the last days, says God, 'That I will pour out of my Spirit on all flesh; your sons and your daughters shall prophesy, your young men shall see visions, your old men shall dream dreams.'"

It wasn't until 2012 that the Lord gave me the green light to put many of my experiences and testimonies of others into this book. When I first set out to start writing this book, as any author would, I tried coming up with a title. I'd often go to my husband, Ed, and ask him how a particular title sounded to him. As I'd press him to be honest, with everything I presented to him, he'd honor my request and reply, "Mmmm…that's kind of cheesy" or "Nope, boring." I was grateful for his candor because his feedback showed me what did and didn't work.

For weeks I struggled to come up with a great title without any luck. It took about a year before I gave in and threw up my hands and prayed, "Lord, I give it all up to You. I'm going to wait for *You* to give me the title for this book."

Immediately after I prayed that prayer, the Lord spoke! He asked four simple words, "What did you see?"

That's all I needed. All I had to do was answer His question.

I replied, "I saw God last night."

Now, I know some will say, "But the Bible says, 'No man has ever seen God'" (John 1:18, Exodus 33:20). Don't be confused, as this is not a contradiction. Since the Bible has proven to be 100 percent infallible and inspired by God Himself, this scripture has to be entirely true.

God is a Trinity and the Bible speaks of three Godheads within the Trinity: the Father, the Son, and the Holy Spirit (1 John 5:7; Matthew 28:19). Since accurate records exist of thousands seeing Jesus, Who *is* God (John 1:1, 14), scripture can't be referring to Him (His part of the Godhead). The Gospel of John clears up that scripture as referring to the Father:

"Not that anyone has seen the Father, except He Who is from God; He has seen the Father" -John 6:46

When my dad and I were having a conversation about this, he reminded me how angels always commanded people not to bow down to them because they are not God, but when people did the same to Jesus, He would by all means allow it, proving His deity.

1

Be Careful What You Bring Into Your Home

AS A LITTLE GIRL, when my mother used to bring me to church, we'd often witness demons being cast out of people, mostly visitors. I remember the pastor yelling to the ushers to grab the children and have them face the wall. We couldn't look on them. My mother tells me that while we faced the wall, someone deeply spiritual would pray over us to protect us from the evil spirits.

At that time in my life, I was clueless as to why our pastor would instruct us to face the wall, especially while service was still going on. As a curious eight year old, I'd slowly turn my head to see what the commotion was all about, sometimes prompting ushers to yell, "Jennifer! Wall!"

So there I stood, yet again, facing a boring, pictureless wall. Had there been stained glass windows or some other sort of intriguing wallpaper pattern we could follow, maybe it would have made staring at the wall a whole lot easier!

One particular time, moments before the "facing of the wall", I, with the witness of an approximate 25-person congregation, saw a 17 year old girl make her way down the altar to give her life to Jesus Christ. Moments before she could make it to the front, she yelled a hellish scream and dashed for the sanctuary exit immediately to the left hand side of the alter. Because our tiny Philadelphia church was renting a room on the second story of a larger church, a balcony stood right off our sanctuary's exit. Right before the girl tried to dive off the balcony, two deacons rushed to close the double doors just in the nick of time. This girl was being possessed by demons and they were trying to kill her by plunging her to her death.

As the pastor grabbed her anointing oil and threw her hands on the erratic girl's forehead, the pastor ordered the ushers to have all the children face the wall. Over the commotion of the crowd, I heard, "In the name of Jesus, Satan I rebuke you! Get out of this girl, by the blood of Jesus! Get out of her! Get out of her now! In Jesus' name!"

We heard the demons inside of her scream a long, drowned out, "Nooo!", but the pastor insisted on rebuking the spirits using Jesus' name. The whole ordeal took about 30 seconds to resolve, and by the time the rest of the children and I could turn back around, the girl was standing with her arms stretched up high, surrendering to the salvation only provided through Jesus Christ.

It wouldn't be until years later that my mother would explain the purpose of distracting the children. She explained that when someone was possessed by demons, once that demon is cast out it needs some other place to go or a being to go into.

It's similar to the time when Jesus cast demons out of two possessed men, and the demons asked Jesus if He *were* to cast them out, if they could be cast into the herd of pigs feeding close by. They were, and the weight of their evil drowned the pigs in a river (Matthew 8:28-34). For this reason, the people of our church didn't want the spirits to jump inside of us.

That was the beginning of my glimpse into the supernatural realm, and boy, was it *real*.

In the early winter of 1997 (I remember the year because that's when the movie *Titanic* was released), I spent the night with a friend from school, named Audrey. She was Asian, and I always liked going over her house because her mother would always make us delicious oriental dishes. Since it wasn't a school night, we stayed up all night watching TV and talking about boys—the basic things teenage girls do at sleepovers.

Just before we were going to "cop-out" for the night, we went through a stack of her boy band posters. Most were of an Asian band that she really liked. She asked me if I wanted one so I said, "Sure." She had maybe four different posters of them, yet *being Audrey*, she gave me the worst poster, the one I didn't want, but I took it to be polite. I immediately became hesitant because in the back of my mind I remembered my pastor always saying, "Be careful what you bring into your house, especially if you have no idea what it stands for." This played over and over in my mind that night.

The next afternoon, grasping the rolled up poster during my 30 minute walk back home, the words of my pastor finally slipped my mind until a couple of minutes before bedtime. I had to decide whether or not to hang the poster.

The apartment my mother, sister, niece and I lived in was the first place we lived after my parents separated, and the bedroom I was given lacked windows and was the size of a rectangular walk-in closet. I had just enough room to fit my bed and retain a narrow walking space.

I had a couple of posters already on my wall—one, I remember being a celebrity "Got Milk" advertisement. I peeled off the corners of that poster to make room for the new one I had just gotten from Audrey. As I unrolled the new poster, I kept going back and forth in my mind whether I should put it up. Still debating myself, I heard my pastor's voice yet again. I felt some sort of warning rising from within me, but I finally decided to go along with it and hang it up figuring, "What the heck! What's the worst that could happen?" Boy was I about to find out.

The poster was up. I had forgotten all about the debating that went on inside of me and focused on how cute the boys on the poster were. As I got ready for bed, I went to my mother's room and let her know I was "hitting the hay" for the night. I closed my door and turned off the light. Not having windows, it was now pitch black in my room. The only light was the light from the bottom crack of the door from the hall light. Thankfully that night, the hall light happened to be left on.

As I lay in bed, I put the sheets over me, closed my eyes and went to sleep. What seemed like two or three hours later, I opened my eyes to find three to four, glowing Asian guys dancing on my wall! I thought I was dreaming, so I closed my eyes, opened them up again to find them *still* there.

There they were, in the exact same spot where I taped the poster—one was playing the drums, the other a guitar and one or two more were dancing. Although they were playing musical instruments, it was completely silent.

It scared the mess out of me and I started to freak out. In slight denial of what my eyes were seeing, I remembered movies I had seen in the past when people would smack themselves to see if they were dreaming or not, so as a last resort, I did, but they were *still* there!

This wasn't a dream and I wasn't going crazy, but rather spirits were literally dancing on my bedroom wall and I wasn't going to stay to see the end of it. With the hall light on I could see exactly where my door was. I darted out of that room like a bat out of you-know-where!

I ran into my mother in the hallway and squealed, "There's spirits dancing on my wall! They're dancing on my wall!" She looked at me like I was out of my mind. I brought her into my room so she could see it for herself, but they were gone.

"Ain't nothin' on your wall," she said. "Honey-child, you need to go to bed."

"Nah-ah!" I rebutted. "I'm not sleeping in there! I'm sleeping *your* room!"

I think I may have slept in my mother's room for a good three months until I got up the courage to sleep a night back in my room. Now as an adult, I'm extremely careful as to what I bring into my home, car or dwelling space, because as I discovered as a child, the supernatural realm exists.

Sorcery in the House

Sara D.
Meriden, CT

When I was 18 years old, I became friends with a girl I met from school, and then later moved in with her and her mother.

One evening, my roommate and I decided to have a few friends over for a Bible study. When everyone arrived, we gathered together to open up in prayer. Smack dab in the middle of the prayer, my roommate suddenly fell to the floor and began to shake violently! A voice from inside of her that *wasn't* her own started to yell and snarl out ghastly and demented locutions. Except for one woman in the house, everyone else was petrified and didn't know what to do because we had never seen anything like it before.

The woman who was unafraid frantically told us not to look at my roommate. She instructed us to keep our eyes closed and pray because the girl was currently demon possessed. The woman then began to rebuke the evil spirits out of the girl using the name of Jesus. Once the spirits were cast out, my roommate explained to us that she and her mother was formerly involved in witchcraft. She described how she was brought up into that lifestyle and how her mother used to perform much sorcery within the house. But one day, her mother decided that she wanted to give up the occult lifestyle for good; therefore, she went to her fellow witches with the news and they refused. In their refusal, they placed numerous curses on her life, health, family, house and all of her possessions, thus, manifesting into what everyone saw that night.

A few weeks passed since the incident at our Bible study, and my roommate decided that it would be a good idea to go to church with me that Sunday. During service, while sitting in the pews of my small, Holy Spirit filled, Spanish church, I noticed the message was really touching the heart of my roommate. When it came time at the end of the service for the Altar Call, she decided *then* was the time to give her life back to Christ. The moment she reached the altar, *the same thing happened all over again*, but this time it was worse! She had even *more* demons this time. The pastor of the church had to cast the spirits out just as the woman at our Bible Study had. <u>Satan was fighting to keep her, but Jesus wanted her more.</u>

After this, my roommate solely gave her life over to the Lord and is now free from demons.

"When an unclean spirit goes out of a man, he goes through dry places, seeking rest, and finds none. Then he says, 'I will return to my house from which I came.' And when he comes, he finds it empty, swept, and put in order. Then he goes and takes with him seven other spirits more wicked than himself, and they enter and dwell there; and the last state of that man is worse than the first." – Matthew 12:43-45

2

God, the Gentleman

GROWING UP I HAD a terrible stutter, all the way from kindergarten through my senior year of high school. Even though I'd stutter to the point where I would cross my eyes and lose my breath, God made sure I never went friendless. Kids will be kids and they'd tease me here and there, but it never got under my skin. I don't think the teasing got to me because I never saw my stuttering as a disability, even though others may have. Because my parents helped me build confidence from an early age, I never let stuttering stop me from being myself and getting to know people.

In seventh grade I had many friends. We valued our friendship so much that we created The Friends Club. This was serious, so serious that we even had matching colored purple pens that hung around our necks so that everyone would know we had a friendship pact. We were a cheerful group known by much of the school as being constant gigglers, which some people found annoying.

One late afternoon at school, after puppeteering practice was over, my friends and I were waiting inside the south side door of the building for our rides. As usual we were giggling and having a good ole' time when my best friend left me alone with a new girl who had just joined the school and our group. We went to gather up our belongings. The girl and I struck up a conversation, I can't remember what about, but it seemed light and harmless. After our little chat, I walked outside of the heavy, steel doors onto the asphalt playground feeling great. I remember thinking about how great my life was and all the friends I had made. I gazed into the beautiful sunset, highlighted by pinks and yellows, lifted my eyes up to God and sincerely, foolishly, said, "God, I don't need You anymore. I have all these friends, so I no longer need You."

It's amazing how we fail to realize that all the good things we have, which we often take for granted, comes from God. That day, I took my God for granted, not appreciating how much of a hand He had on my life and the blessing of friendships that He had bestowed on me.

After my little, self-important speech to God, I turned around and walked back toward the stone-walled school building. The very moment I opened the door, I was bombarded with angry screams and false accusations. I couldn't believe it!

I was totally shocked and confused as to what was going on. My best friend accused me of calling her names behind her back. Still confused, I asked her what she was talking about and who was telling her these lies. She pointed to the new girl and said her name. The girl who I was just having a friendly conversation with had fabricated an entire lie about me while I was outside telling God to "take a hike."

God, being a gentleman, didn't force me to appreciate Him, love Him or value Him; therefore, He honored my request (especially because it had come from the heart.)

I'll never forget that day, because that's when I realized that God really does hear our prayers; He really does respect us and our wishes, and more than anything, He makes such a significant impact in our lives when His hand is on something *and when it is removed.*

I took God for granted that day and paid the cost dearly. Not only did I lose my best friend, but the rest of my friends despised me, the entire class shunned me, the teachers turned on me and for the first time ever, I was absolutely friendless—not because of the lie the new girl had told, but because God was the Perfect Gentleman and honored my request. The Lord gave and took away (Job 1:21).

God is not a dictator; He does not force us to love Him. Coercion isn't true love. We'd be like robots serving Him without sincerity. He does not force us to serve, honor, nor obey Him; that comes by freewill. Despite this, He is an ultimatum God when it comes to our life.

If you were to put it in "Layman's Terms," it would be: Live your life however you choose, but before you die, you must accept Jesus as your Savior, the *Only*, True God, or that's it. The tie is cut forever. The problem is, since you have no clue *when* you will die, it's best to come to Him *now* so you and He will never part (2 Corinthians 6:2).

I completely understand why God puts it this way, because life without Him is downright awful. He only took His hand off a piece of my life and my social life went down the drain in a matter of seconds—which is devastating for a teenager.

Let's look at the story of Samson, the strongest man who ever lived. The Bible says His strength was in his hair and he was never to cut it. Each time the Spirit of the Lord came upon Samson, he, being one man, protected all of Israel from the Philistines for 20 years, killed a lion with his bare hands, and killed 1,000 men with the jawbone of a donkey. Yet Samson, being human and therefore foolish, eventually disobeyed God, gave into temptation, admitting to Delilah (a woman he desired) that cutting his hair would take his strength away. While he slept in her lap, she chopped off his seven locks, and when he awoke, the Bible says the Lord left him and he didn't even know it! God's hand was no longer on him and for the first time, Samson had the strength of the average man. He was captured, had his eyes gouged out, was chained up, made a fool of, and later died, killing the Philistines with the bit of strength He asked God to give him one last time (Judges 13-16).

We *need* God! We need every bit of Him and all that He has to offer and is willing to give to us, because without Him, we are nothing and have nothing good (James 1:17). If we don't want Him, since He is the Perfect Gentleman, He'll honor our wishes.

Saved From Custody

Justus K.
Bungoma, Kenya

In 2003, the Government of Kenya, through the Ministry of Transport, instituted a law on public transport. Passengers were to wear seatbelts, and if you were found not wearing one, you could be taken to court and fined or imprisoned.

One day, I was traveling from my village home to our nearby town to transfer ownership of the parcel of land we had bought for our church. We boarded a taxi at our market centre to town. Along the way, we were met with law enforcers who stopped our taxi for inspection. There were many vehicles there which had been impounded.

At the same place was a madman with his luggage. He took a small Bible from his luggage and asked one policeman to read it for him as we were listening, waiting to be inspected. The passage he read from was Luke 3:14, but the madman started expounding on the scriptures against the law enforcers who were extorting bribes from the vehicle owners. The policemen were so intimidated by the preaching of the madman that they started to chase him away. We burst out in laughter due to the drama. The anger of the policemen was turned to us and they arrested us for not wearing seatbelts.

When we were taken to the Bungoma Police Station, the police took us to the jail cells, without booking us—which is against the law. In the cells, we met people with different criminal offenses, so they started beating us-which is common in our Kenyan cells. One man came to me and slapped me in the face. As I turned holding my cheek due to pain, another man recognized me and asked me what a pastor has done to be brought to custody. Before I could answer, another gave a Bible to me to preach and pray for their release. I just held the Bible but never uttered a word. I told them that I was in custody as a law breaker not as a preacher.

When I told them what happened, one man woke up and slapped the man who had slapped me. Suddenly, they started exchanging fists! The fight got so bad that it caused the police to come into the cells to ask "what was up". They were told, "How one dared to slap the man of God?"

The law enforcers calmed the cells and went away. After 20 minutes or so, it erupted *again*; this time almost everyone in the cells was involved, apart from me. The police came back for the second time and after hearing the cause, the prisoners demanded that the pastor (me) be removed from the cells or they would do more harm.

They called the officer in charge of the police station who wanted to know what was going on. When he was told the situation, he commanded I be removed from custody and be released. I was let go without any charges held against me!

I really saw God come to my rescue.

"Peter was therefore kept in prison, but constant prayer was offered to God for him by the church. And when Herod was about to bring him out, that night Peter was sleeping, bound with two chains between two soldiers; and the guards before the door were keeping the prison. Now behold, an angel of the Lord stood by him, and a light shone in the prison; and he struck Peter on the side and raised him up, saying, "Arise quickly!" And his chains fell off his hands. Then the angel said to him, "Gird yourself and tie on your sandals"; and so he did. And he said to him, "Put on your garment and follow me." So he went out and followed him, and did not know that what was done by the angel was real, but thought he was seeing a vision. When they were past the first and the second guard posts, they came to the iron gate that leads to the city,

which opened to them of its own accord; and they went out and went down one street, and immediately the angel departed from him." -Acts 12:5-10

3

On My Way to Hell with Religion as My Guide

TRAILING BEHIND MY BIG sister, Leslie, I made my way to the altar at the age of eight to give my heart to Jesus. And for years that became my pride. I'd go around boasting, "I've been saved since I was eight!" That sort of became my trophy for a long time. Instead of giving glory to Jesus Christ for His painful sacrifice on the cross for my salvation, I'd give it to myself for becoming born again at such a young age.

When I was around 17 years old, I was given a dream that shook me to the core. I dreamt I was joyriding in a car with two other friends in the backseat, and I was the driver. Then I foolishly yelled to them, "Let's drive into a wall!" Strangely enough, they gladly accepted. The first wall I could find was a red bricked wall and I drove head-on into it. I didn't feel a thing. I just remember being instantly in a different location other than Earth; I was in Hell. I don't know how I knew, but I just knew it, and I was being nailed to a cross, hanging upright in a very bright, white room. With my arms outstretched with no control over my body, I could hear the thick and heavy thuds of hammers banging into my hands simultaneously, but I couldn't feel anything (more than likely because it was a dream). I tried to look over to see who was hammering the nails but I couldn't, I just knew that there was more than one unpleasant being mercilessly banging into my hands. I suppose my feet had already been nailed or tied because I briefly remember them being bound together at the bottom.

What gripped me the most was that, there was also an *absolute* knowing I had that Jesus was *also* present in the room. So I turned my head to the left, as far as I could to see Jesus, but I couldn't. I began to wail and cried out to Him, "...but Jesus, I love You." Then He walked over from my left and stood directly in front of me. I still couldn't see His face, yet I knew it was Him. He answered these three words I will never forget, "No. You don't." Then I woke up.

The very next day, I remember getting onto the school bus telling my best friend about the dream, afterward promising I'd never sin again. I realized I was lying. What a contradiction. I didn't get the dream. I just held on to Jesus' words when I told Him I loved Him. It shocked and hurt me when He told me I didn't. So I told a close relative of mine the dream and what Jesus said, and they responded, "Jesus would never say that! That's not right!" Without even realizing it, I responded, "Jesus tells it like it is. He can't lie!" And it was in that moment that I questioned all my years of being a "Christian". Was I really a Christian or was I just a "holy-rollie" beating people with the Bible? If I died today, would I really miss Heaven and end up in Hell? And most of all, the biggest question was: Did I *really* love Jesus?

A few months later in my high school science class, a friend who was sitting across from me laughed and said to me, "Jenny, you're so funny." I questioned her, and she replied, "You're just hilarious! When people say they don't believe in Jesus, you just get mad and say, 'Oh well, you're just going to Hell, then!'" And when she said that, it was as if all of time had stopped. I saw my friend almost fall on the floor laughing, but it was as if her laughter was put on mute. I was cut to the heart, realizing Jesus was *nothing* like that. Jesus never got mad at people if they didn't believe He was the Son of God. He never blew the final whistle as I had and damned someone to

Hell. He didn't give up on them. He'd tell them the truth in love, stating, "I am the Way, the Truth, and the Life. No man comes to the Father but by Me (John 14:6)." Jesus had already planted the seed—either people would accept or reject. If they rejected, that was on them. But He always left the door open for repentance and Truth (Matthew 4:17, John 8:11).

Still in the moment, I suddenly saw a slideshow in my mind of all the times I'd verbally attack someone if they didn't agree with me about Jesus, or the times I'd curse others to Hell for not believing. I knew my friend thought I'd laugh along with her, but I didn't. It was then that I felt a deep remorse for how I treated people, having the audacity to falsely represent Jesus in such a heartless and crude way. I became the poster child for 1 Corinthians 13:1 and 3b:

"Though I speak with the tongues of men and angels, but have not love, I have become sounding brass or a clanging cymbal...it profits me nothing!"

The concluding revelation I got from this, which took the scales from my eyes was this:

Jesus was *nothing* like that. I was a religious *nut!* There was no love within me for the people, just a condemning spirit making a whole lot of noise. How many lives did I scare away from knowing Jesus? I cannot count.

About ten years later, the dream I had years prior was still in the back of my mind. Although the dream changed my life (for the better), I still couldn't figure out why the room in my dream was so bright, being that I was being nailed to a cross in *Hell.* I pondered this for a long time, until one day in church, a pastor read an insert of Bill Wiese's book, *23 Minutes In Hell.* As the pastor read this man's testimony of experiencing literal Hell, it gripped my attention, as well as everyone else's in the room. Then I said to myself, I'll really believe him if he mentions people hung on crosses down there. And lo and behold, he did! Nearly towards the end of his experience in Hell, he explained how he suddenly saw a bright light that filled his entire space, and the light was coming from Jesus Christ, coming to remove him from that ghastly place.

I was thrilled at this point. Not only did I get confirmation about the crosses, but I also got revelation about why it was so bright in the room. It came to my realization that the reason why it was so bright in my dream, being in Hell, was because Jesus was with me. *He was the Light (John 8:12, John 1:6-9)!* I now know that He gave me this surreal dream because He wanted to open my eyes to what a *real and true* Christian is—someone who follows and obeys Jesus Christ, living the life, understanding He is without limit in deed, in action, and in self, and *has a personal relationship with Him.*

Relationship was the part I had completely skipped, being full of rules that come with religion. Jesus never called us to religion, but rather, a relationship with Him (Revelation 3:20; Matthew 11:28).

Wildfire

Gloria N.
Waterbury, CT

In the beginning week of July 2012, I dreamt of being somewhere in a country setting. It was very beautiful and was summer out. I was in the middle of the road and there were a lot of people looking in front of them, afraid because police blocked the entry to a forest reserve. The officers then put up yellow caution tape. As I was in shock by what I was seeing, all of a sudden, everything around went silent. I saw people scared, crying and screaming. Then, out of nowhere, everyone left except for the officers and fire department.

I looked over and saw Jesus standing to my right. I said to Him, "Lord, what are You doing here?"

He turned, looked at me and said, "Daughter, do you see what is happening? No one believes anymore. They don't believe in My coming."

I was in complete and utter shock and didn't know how to respond to Him. As He continued to talk, He started to cry and sob like a baby. My heart was broken because I tried to hug Him, but He sort of curled up into a ball with me.

He said, "My Daughter, the people don't believe that I'm coming. They don't believe. A lot of people are lost. It hurts Me to see them this way."

I asked Him, "What can I do?"

Jesus stood up straight, wiped his tears away and said, "Alert them!" His voice sounded sad and mad at the same time. Again He boldly said, "<u>Alert them!</u> All the signs are here. <u>The seven seals are about to break!</u>"

"I will," I said.

When I said that, He turned, looked at me and responded, "Hurry! Tell them. Let them know, but remember they are going to judge and criticize! Don't worry, I will be with you. Don't worry because they judged and criticized *Me*. Run, please! My daughter, tell the church and the people that my coming is near, and those who don't believe, their judgment will come." Then He said, "Look!"

Obeying Him, I looked up and I saw a big angel flying down from Heaven with a speed not of this world, blowing a golden trumpet. As the angel drew closer, it turned into fire and flew into the forest reserve. The forest lit up in fire and the firefighters weren't able to control it. I was again in shock!

When I turned to look at Jesus, He said to me, "You see, the end is near. Go, run; tell them I'm coming!"

Nervously, I replied, "Okay, Lord. I'll go."

He said, "Okay, run and remember My daughter, *you* need to get ready as well, because I'm coming for you."

Jesus looked at me, smiled, then gave me a hug and a kiss on the cheek, and then He left.

When I awoke, the first thing I noticed was that the television was left on the Weather Channel. They were talking about a fire in Colorado that grew to 90% over night and was uncontrollable. That's when I knew, and still know 'til this day, even telling my family and friends, that I had this dream at the start of the catastrophic 2012 Colorado Wildfires! That's when it hit me that it is written that God will "make His power known" (Romans 9:22).

Take notice that there weren't any reports of animal deaths in the fire. Why? Because it's their animal instinct to flee when they feel danger is near! JESUS IS COMING!

"How great are His signs, and how mighty His wonders!"
–Daniel 4:3

4

The Name of Jesus Is Literal Power

WHEN I WAS 17, my mother, niece and I went to a friend's house from church for a little picnic. Folks sat around laughing, eating and enjoying each other's fellowship. Compliments were heaped on the guy on the grill for how tasty the food was, and they were encouraging him to take a break and eat. He refused, explaining that for some strange reason, it's difficult for him to eat his own food. It must be a psychological thing because I get the same way when I make certain dishes.

At the picnic was Mr. Mike, a very large man with a strong, baritone voice. When he spoke, it sounded as if he were speaking into a microphone. He was very friendly and sociable, interacting with everyone. As we all sat in a circle on white, folding chairs, enjoying our barbecue, I glanced past everyone's head, eyeing an oddly shaped, yet unique-looking car in the distance. The car was gray with two doors and had slightly red-tinted windows. It intrigued me.

I blurted out, "Wow! What kind of car is that?"

"You like that car?" Mr. Mike asked. "That's mine."

"Really? It's cool," I complimented. "What kind of car *is* that?"

I had never seen a car like Mr. Mike's in my life, or if I had, I must have never paid it any attention.

"Well, Jenny," Mr. Mike started in his deep voice, "It's a 1988 Saab 900 Turbo. It's got red seats. You want it?"

"Really?" I squealed. My mom's eyes got huge and she almost dropped her plate in shock.

"You got your license?" he asked.

"No, but I will on my 18th birthday."

"I tell you what, when you get your license, that car is yours," Mr. Mike promised me. "I've gotta fix up a few things on it first, then I'll give it to ya!"

I was so grateful. This was going to be my very first car and I felt so blessed that Mr. Mike would be so generous to *give* me his Saab...for free!

November came around. It was days before my 18th birthday when I saw Mr. Mike at church. I asked him if he was still serious about giving me his car, and he assured me he was.

I told him I was getting my license on my birthday, and he said, "Then that's the day I'll give you the car, but I still have a couple of things I need to do to it first." Then he scratched his head, "But Jenny, how do you know you're gonna pass? I can't give you the car unless you pass."

I told him, "Don't worry, Mr. Mike. I'm speaking it into existence and Jesus is gonna be with me, so I can't fail! You'll see."

My birthday arrived and so did the big test. Because the state of Connecticut requires a written test along with the road test, I studied for weeks to memorize all the ins and outs. So when I arrived at the DMV, I was extremely confident I was going to pass.

My number was called and I walked into a room where they had an open computer ready for me. To my recollection, I was only permitted to get four questions wrong and still be able to pass the written test, but being naïve, I figured, "No big deal. It'll be a walk in the park."

Question number one, I got wrong. Question number four, I got wrong. It wasn't as easy as I thought. By the time I got to question number seven, I had already maxed out all four, permissible, wrong answers. One more incorrect answer meant I would fully flunk my driver's test...on my *birthday*! I began to panic and sweat. I thought

47

about that car and everyone I told that I was going to pass without a doubt. The pressure mounted as I proceeded.

Finally, I made it to the very last question. The panic started again. I had to get this question right or else I was done. So, I did what I should have remembered to do at the beginning of the test, and that was to pray. Under my breath I muttered, "Jesus, please, please help me! I need You!"

The final question went something like this: "When driving, what do you do if a car is merging onto the highway and you're in the right lane?"

My prayer worked! That was the very question my future sister-in-law (at the time) asked me right before I headed out the door to take the test.

I answered her, "Speed up?"

She said, "No, you merge over to the left lane."

That was how I passed the written exam. If I hadn't prayed, and if God hadn't allowed my sister-in-law to give me a final word of knowledge, I wouldn't have passed the test!

The driving test went flawlessly and I was now cruising in my 1988 Saab 900. As the months went by, the car still needed a bit more work done to it, but in the meantime, I kept driving it because that was my only transportation to my telemarketing job in the rural town next to mine.

Being that it was winter in New England, that year, it seemed as if every week we were getting slammed with snow. My transmission was starting to go, so my car was only capable of driving forward, but not in reverse.

My Saturday morning shift had ended and I was heading back home. On the way, I missed a turn. Because my car wasn't capable of going backwards, I had to find a cul-de-sac or street wide enough to allow me to do a complete circle and turn around.

To my left, I quickly spotted a little cul-de-sac down a short, tiny road down a slight hill. I made the turn, drove slowly down the hill and found myself surrounded by four or five big, beautiful houses on acres and acres of land. As I made my way around the tiny cul-de-sac, I hit the gas to gain momentum to make it back up the small hill but the car spun in place and rolled back down the hill. I needed new tires for the winter because my traction was almost non-existent! It was one of two major issues I needed fixed, but I was a young, inexperienced girl who rode the transit bus all her life and knew nothing about cars and their upkeep.

I made several attempts to get up that stubborn hill but all I got was the smell of burnt tires. At that point, I had been stuck for about 20 minutes. Brainstorming on how to get out of that place, I considered knocking on someone's door and asking them for help, but when I reached for my door handle, I realized cows, horses and chickens surrounded my car! They were all eyeballing me so I started to panic a little. I quickly took my hand off that handle and said to myself, "There's *no way* I'm getting out of this car now!"

You see, I was raised in the city, and the only animals I was used to seeing roam free were alley cats, stray dogs and pigeons. So for me, this experience was like being thrown into the *Twilight Zone*.

"What do I do? What do I do?" I thought as I gripped the wheel. All of a sudden, it came to me. It was something I should have done from the very beginning— pray.

I took one last look at those animals, grabbed onto the wheel, hit the gas and yelled, "Jesus!" for as long as I could. As I yelled His name with my foot flooring the gas pedal and tires spinning, I felt my car inching up the hill as if it was literally being pulled. Within seconds I was back on top of the hill!

There's just *something* about the name of Jesus.

* * *

One night, I dreamt I was in the wing entrance of a mall. Feeling a presence behind me, I turned around. Before me stood a man, staring at me. As I began to walk, I could hear him following me, so again I turned around. I instantly knew that he was not of God. The man approached me with sinister eyes. I shouted, "I rebuke you in the name of Jesus! By the blood of Jesus I rebuke you, Satan!"

Immediately when I rebuked him, a dagger appeared in my left hand. As he came within arm's reach I pierced him in his stomach, then ran away as fast as my legs could carry me. The man began to lose strength but still he came after me, yet growing weaker by the second. Noticing he wasn't giving up, I turned and pierced him again in the midsection once more. So determined was this man, that he began assaulting any innocent bystanders who got between us. There was much screaming and commotion throughout the mall, but the man was now terribly weak, almost to the point of death.

By the time I reached the other end of the mall, the man had vanished. I stood with the dagger still in my hand. This dagger, I *knew*, was special.

When I woke up from the dream, I asked the Lord to interpret it for me. He said, "My name is a weapon to the Devil." I asked Him why a dagger showed up in my hand and He revealed to me that it wasn't until I used the name "Jesus" that He gave me a weapon to defend myself against the enemy and never was the enemy able to harm me.

If you think about it, sometimes the enemy is so ruthless that he will sometimes try to hurt anyone he can who gets in his path of destroying you.

***

Back in 2002, my friend Dana and I went to a carnival that stopped by our town every year for a week. Everyone deemed the carnival cursed because it always seemed to rain when it came to our town, but this year, it didn't.

Dana and I had just gotten off our work shift at Walgreens, and the carnival happened to be right across the street. I'll admit, I'm a scaredy-cat when it comes to roller coasters and thrill rides, but I had the time of my life when Dana talked me into going onto "The Zipper," a vertically-shaped, oblong ride with freestyle, flipping cages. I don't know how she talked me into getting into that cage, but she did, and we had a hilarious time!

Since Dana was a "girly girl," her purse was filled with cosmetics of every kind and coins, lots and lots of coins. While on the ride, it wasn't until the cage started to flip with us, being at least 50 feet in the air, that Dana realized she had forgotten to zip up her purse. The both of us had to find this out the hard way! All I remember was us screaming, not just because we were being flipped and tossed around in mid air, but because we were getting whacked in the face by lipsticks, mascara, perfume, mirrors and oh yeah, coins…lots and lots of coins! We had to have been on that ride four or five minutes, but it seemed like 30 because the man who controlled the ride kept adding and subtracting people to the ride, but seemed to forget to subtract *us*. It wasn't until Dana yelled at him to let us off that we were finally freed, but by that time, we were still buzzing from the fun time we had.

After the carnival, we took the transit bus home because neither of us had a license at the time. We were the only people on the bus until the bus driver picked up a couple from our town's movie theater.

The man who got on was in his late 30s to early 40s, and was out-of-his-mind drunk, which right away made me very uncomfortable. The first time I ever saw an intoxicated person was when I was around nine or 10 years old, and my Uncle Bruce had driven my tipsy great-uncle over to a Thanksgiving dinner. He was extremely drunk and acting erratic, which scared the mess out of me because my parents weren't drinkers and alcohol was never allowed into my home. So, I did what any frightened child would do; I ran and hid. Somehow I just knew it wasn't natural or normal because he wasn't in his right state of mind.

So when this man got onto the bus, Dana and I were at the very front of the bus facing each other, she on one side and I on the other, which made it easier for us to talk to each other. The drunken man's girlfriend sat in the mid-section of the bus but he oddly chose to plop right on down right next to Dana. At first I thought they knew each other by the way he was acting towards her, but when I noticed the discomfort on her face, I got the clue and asked her if she knew him. She said, "No."

The man kept touching her and putting his arm around her, slurring "mumble-jumble" in her face with his liquor breath. I wanted to help my friend but didn't know what to do. I was only a teenager and this was a grown man. I didn't know how I could stop him. The bus driver completely ignored the situation and his girlfriend just sat there laughing.

I began to pray, "Lord, use me. Please, use me."

Suddenly, a supernatural boldness came upon me and words shot out of my mouth that I had no control over. I pointed to the man, looked deep into his eyes and boldly shouted, "Satan, I know who you are! Come out of this man in the name of Jesus! I bind you by the blood of Jesus Christ! I rebuke you! Come out, in Jesus' name!"

The whole bus went silent. All anyone could hear was the engine running. The bus driver nearly froze at the wheel and the drunk man's girlfriend looked at him as if she was thinking, "Uh oh, you've done it now!"

At this point, I was fearless, as I knew I had on the Full Armor of God, as mentioned in Ephesians 6:10-18. Shaken, the man replied, "Man, I'm sorry. I didn't mean any harm. I'm really sorry. I didn't mean to hurt anybody. Please forgive me." His slur was entirely gone and he *immediately* reverted back into sobriety! The man had detoxed in an *instant*.

I must admit, it surprised me at how powerful the name of Jesus truly was (and is). It was as if Satan put his tail between his legs and ran off like the coward that he is when I used the name of Jesus against him.

✳ Although the name of Jesus is extremely powerful, it is *not* to be played around with and used for personal gain because it will not work and could very well be used *against* you. The Holy Spirit *must* be within you and it's crucial that you speak it with authority over the enemy (Satan and his demons).

Here's a great example: When the Apostle Paul, the converted "bad boy" of the Bible, was performing miracles, healing the sick and casting out evil spirits by the power of God in the name of Jesus (for God's Kingdom), seven vagabonds saw what Paul was doing, approached a demon-possessed man and tried mimicking what was being done, but they were not of God and tried using the name of Jesus for their own personal gain and show. So when the evil spirit that was in the demon possessed man spoke to the vagabonds, it said, *"Jesus I know, Paul I know; but who are you?"* The Bible goes on to say that the spirit in the man leapt on them, stripped the men naked and beat

Speak God's name with authority.

them! Fear fell on everyone who was there and *the name of the Lord Jesus was magnified* (Acts 19:12-17).

✳︎   In other words you, yourself, have absolutely no power over Satan unless God lives inside of you. It is not *you* who Satan fears, but the God *in* you. Those who have Christ living inside of them are a walking force against the Kingdom of Hell. But if you do not have Christ within you, do not attempt to battle the devil because you will lose!

Just think, if you've ever seen exorcists in scary movies or elsewhere, what are the two things they always bring with them? The Holy Bible and the cross of Jesus Christ! You never see them bring any other book from any other religion because they know what works. The name of Jesus works! God's Word works! But even still, if those people are doing it for the wrong reason, it will only work against them. His name is not to be played with. It is meant to be respected.

Those who have christ living inside of them are a walking force against the Kingdom of hell.

Stop the Rain

Simone F.
Wichita, KS

I learned how to rebuke storms and how powerful praise was against Satan and his dark kingdom. When you feed on the Word and have a keen understanding of the Word of God, you begin to know your power in the Lord.

One time, I commanded rain to stop after it had been raining for 30 days straight (not 40)! You see, my husband was a painter and couldn't work because of it, and all of my neighbors were getting their basements flooded; therefore, I felt it was imperative that I enforce what God had put on my heart to do. Rebuke it!

I felt a righteous fury well up inside my soul and spirit and commanded the rain to stop in the name of *Jesus*. A few minutes after I had done so, it completely stopped and didn't rain for months following.

Later, I went on to rebuke tornadoes using that matchless and powerful name of Jesus, sending them on their way and seeing them lose power in seconds—dissipating into nothing.

"Then Joshua spoke to the LORD in the day when the LORD delivered up the Amorites before the children of Israel, and he said in the sight of Israel, 'Sun, stand still over Gibeon; and Moon, in the Valley of Aijalon.' So the sun stood still, and the moon stopped." -Joshua 10:12-13b

5

When We Held Hands

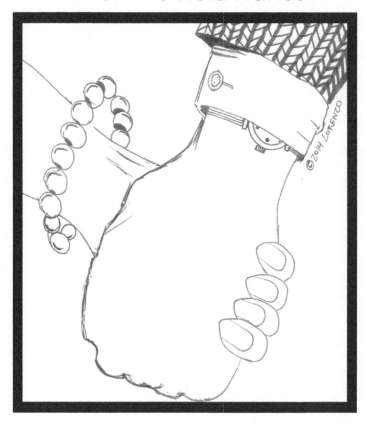

BY 2004, I HAD been married to my husband, Ed, for a year and a half. While he'd be out working, I'd often sit in our small, 700 square foot apartment in Silverdale, Washington, watching the TBN station on cable.

As I was watching that network one day, on the screen stood a middle-aged, Middle Eastern-looking man, with salt-and-pepper colored hair and a thick Israeli accent. While I watched his show, I was fascinated because he was doing something with the power of God that I had never seen done before. The man would sweep his hands up in the air before a huge throng of thousands of people and shout, "Jesus!" The moment his hands went up, rows of people would fall to the ground like dominoes. I was truly fascinated. I had never seen God work through a person in such a fashion.

I called my mom and rambled on about what I saw on television. She told me his name was Benny Hinn and that "he has the gift of healing." Silly me asked her what she meant by that, and she said, "God gives him the gift to heal people from all sorts of diseases from all over the world. He's known for performing miracles."

From then on, I was hooked! I'd watch Benny Hinn whenever he'd come on television just to see people get healed from being lame, crippled, deaf, dumb, blind and everything else one could think of. It was amazing to me. I loved to hear the testimonies.

Children who were brought up on the huge podiums really intrigued me. There they were, noticeably disabled or in wheelchairs, and sometimes with Benny not even touching them, but rather saying, "Touch," the children were instantly healed. It was beautiful to see parents weeping with joy over their child's miraculous healing.

I made up in my mind that the next time Benny Hinn would come to Washington State, I'd attend one of his crusades. Within a year and a half, however, my husband and I had moved from our one bedroom apartment to Naval housing, had our first child and Benny still wasn't scheduled to come to Washington.

Another year and a half later, we moved back to Connecticut and I forgot about the miracle services until my husband and I bought our first house. Then my memory bank started working again. I began watching his show, *This Is Your Day,* whenever it came on.

Finally, in August of 2011, I took notice that Benny was coming to my hometown of Philadelphia in November and boy was I excited! I called Ed right away and told him we were going; it wasn't even an *option* in my mind. The fact that I had been waiting seven years to go to one of these crusades, and it was happening less than four hours away put me on cloud nine. I couldn't wait for that amazing experience of feeling God heavily in the atmosphere.

With the crusade soon approaching, I requested seats using the ministry's online service and we received the free admission tickets in the mail a few weeks later. We were told to arrive two hours early because people were coming from all over America and the world for these specific crusades.

The day finally arrived! We loaded the kids into the car at my uncle's house in South Jersey where we lodged the night before, stopping in on our drive from Connecticut. In the car, on the way to Philly, I kept going over and over in my head how long I'd waited just to experience what other people at these miracle crusades had been experiencing. It felt surreal, but I savored the anticipation.

Pulling up to Deliverance Evangelistic Church on West Lehigh Avenue, the parking lot was jam-packed, so we had to find a parking spot along a neighborhood street.

It became frustrating because only one-way streets bordered the perimeter of the church, and we kept getting yelled at by onlookers to drive down the right direction, but we got a nice chuckle out of it. We finally found a spot near the McDonald's up the street, not too far from the church.

Walking up the driveway, we saw people from all different nationalities, cultures, even religions (noticeably because of their attire) walking in or being dropped off at the front door. We also couldn't help but notice many sickly, crippled and handicapped people being helped out of vehicles or escorted up the sidewalk and guided into the church.

By the time we entered the building, we were one and a half hours early instead of two because of the parking situation, but didn't mind since the kids weren't yet complaining of being hungry or bored. We made sure to pack snacks and little activities because we knew it could be a long day for them and they were still so small.

When the service began, we joined in praise and worship, singing many hymns I had learned as a child. Mid-song, Benny Hinn walked out and began waving his arms in the air as if he was directing a choir. From the moment his microphone was turned on, he started singing along with the rest of the congregation, but he took the lead. I couldn't figure out why he kept changing songs every minute or so. I told my husband, "We didn't even finish the first one yet!" I just couldn't figure out why we were changing songs so often; we had to have at least sung about 20 different songs in a 30-minute time span (or at least it felt that way).

Many people were waving their hands in the air in surrendering worship, others were crying, dancing and clapping—it was turning into something beautiful. The worship became pure and selfless. The words of every song we sang solely exalted the greatness of God.

Immediately after praise and worship was over, Benny announced that if anyone was healed during praise and worship, to form a line on both sides of the altar. The altar and sanctuary was very big, so two lines had to be formed, one on each side.

"*That* was it?" I thought. "*That's* how it's done? But he didn't even lay hands on anyone or touch anyone." It was very different from what I had assumed how healing would be done.

Ed and I recognized a little, old, crippled woman who we saw being helped out of a vehicle when we were entering into the building. She was standing upward in line, not only standing—walking perfectly! It was very moving because we would see the tears of the family members who joined their loved ones on stage as a witness to their healing.

A Filipino mother and daughter had walked up onto the stage crying. Benny asked them why they were crying, and the daughter, who looked to be in her mid to late 20s said, "My mother and I have driven a very long way to be in one of your conferences. My mother doesn't speak English so I'll have to translate for her. My mother was completely deaf in one ear so it was very difficult for her to hear. But during worship, her ear opened up!"

"Just like that?" Benny asked.

"Yes, just like that!" the daughter cried.

The sincerity and overwhelming gladness that this mother and daughter were experiencing because of the miracle was more than just heartwarming; it softened my heart to the realization of how active God really is. It was humbling. Doubt can be a cinder block wall restraining God from blessing you and giving you His will "as it is in Heaven" (Matthew 6:10).

Benny Hinn continued the service, breaking it down into two short sermons: Salvation and the Importance of

Communion. As he preached on salvation, I realized that I had never been to a service or, for that matter, anywhere else where people of different religions and faiths came running down to an altar *in* their actual religious attire to give their life to Christ!

Just picture it: A person enters into a Christian church out of curiosity or realizing "there must be more to life," decked out in *their own* religious attire, then suddenly, upon hearing the truth about Jesus and that He's the only God who loves them unconditionally, they run down the church altar, pushing past the ushers and congregation. It took me aback. Not only was it cool, I was speechless at how Jesus easily won them over.

As the end of the service approached, Benny announced that he wanted to pray for the youth. Now, by this time my two young children, ages two and five at the time, had gotten very cranky, hungry and tired as we had been there for quite some time; so honestly, I was growing extremely annoyed from the whining. So when Benny said to bring all the youth to the front for prayer, I drug my children as far up to the front of the altar as I could get them because my nerves were frayed! There had to have been hundreds of youth up there, from infants to early 20s.

As the three of us stood there, I thought, "I've got these kids up here because they need prayer and because they keep whining and driving me nuts! Now, *I* need a double dose of prayer *because* I'm going nuts!"

Standing shoulder-to-shoulder in a huge throng, I made sure to hold on to the girls, one in each hand. Ed waited back in the pews because I darted out too quickly for him to realize that we had even gone anywhere!

Benny asked everyone standing in the front to join hands, so we did. The choir finished a song when he said something like, "The choir is going to sing this song again, and when they hit the high note on 'Hallelujah' (or something like that), the Holy Spirit is going to sweep through the people!" He reminded us again to hold hands. The choir began to sing for around 20 to 30 seconds, then the very moment they hit the high note, Benny shouted, "There it is!"

I thought nonchalantly, "Where?"

All of a sudden I saw his hand pointed towards the left side of the room. People were falling down in waves (John 18:6), in a domino effect. The next thing I know, my two year old falls to the ground! Traveling from her hand to mine was a supernatural, [painless] electricity that flowed from my right arm, while a sort of physical, solid wind (it's hard to describe because it was a feeling, a touch, that wasn't of this world) rolled across my stomach, and pushed me down! I squealed like a little girl. There's no way anyone could remain standing with a push like that.

Before I hit the ground, the electricity flowed out from my left arm and into my five year old giving her the same effect—all of which happened within a split second.

Young people were sprawled all over the floor, laid out under the awesome weight of the Holy Spirit. I heard many speaking in tongues and praising God. I looked to my right to make sure my youngest was okay and she was, then I looked to my left at my oldest daughter. I noticed a teenager around 18 years of age had fallen on her, so she was crying, "I wanna go home! I wanna go home!" I asked her if she was hurt and she said, "No."

When the service was over, while we were looking for our car, Ed and I heard a couple of women behind us saying, "Did you feel that wind?" I knew exactly what they were talking about and it *wasn't* the wind outside. I turned around and we began gushing over the supernatural power of God and how physical it was.

After I was done quick-chatting with the women, my family and I crossed the street and finally located our car parked on a side street. After we buckled the girls in their car seats and then buckled *ourselves*, I looked back at our oldest daughter and asked, "Honey, did you like it?" She just looked at me. I asked her again, "Honey, did you like it?"

She said, "Jesus needs to tell me sorry!"

I was confused, so I asked her, "Why does Jesus need to tell you sorry?"

Her response blew me away. She said, "Because He pushed me!"

Ed and I both looked at each other with our jaws dropped. All the while, we thought she was crying because a person had fallen on her, but that wasn't the case. You see, even children recognize the glory of God, more so than most adults, and that was made clear that evening.

That memorable November night God gave me four revelations:

✳ 1.) He revealed to me that it is important to hold hands while we pray because the Holy Spirit will sometimes manifest and physically travel from one person to another while hands are being held in Jesus' name. In doing so, His glory is put to work in everyone who is linked.

2.) I learned that people raise their hands in the air during praise and worship because they're surrendering to the Lord. (I personally never raised my hands during worship until I received this revelation because I didn't understand the reasoning.)

3.) The reason why everyone fell down at the altar was because when the Holy Spirit made Himself manifested, we were unable to withstand Him in all His splendor and glory.

4.) When we worship, Heaven is literally opened up above us and His miracles and wonders are poured onto all who receive it.

***

One spring morning, my friend Esther invited a friend and me over for prayer. I gladly accepted and we met in her basement. Esther and I both had little ones so we had them play in a room adjacent to where we were so we could keep a close eye on them. While the children were playing, the three of us women started talking about how God works in the supernatural. We began sharing experiences we previously had had or *wanted* to have. Before we began to pray, I asked that we join hands because of the power that comes with it, and they gladly accepted.

Esther prayed first, then her friend, and then it was my turn. Esther was holding my left hand while her friend was holding my right. I was expecting something from the Lord since we had just gotten done swooning over His works and wonders (He likes that).

As I began to pray with my eyes closed, I suddenly felt both Esther and her friend's hand enlarge, but I couldn't stop praying! My mouth was moving but my mind was racing; the hands I was now holding had to have been about five inches thick—they were huge! I could feel the Holy Spirit all inside of me. I wanted to open my eyes to look at these hands, but I've learned from past experiences to take my hands off the steering wheel when God is in the driver's seat, so I kept them closed. Still praying, not realizing what I was saying because I was still in awe of what was occurring, all I could hear was the women agreeing with me, "Yes, Lord...In Jesus' name...Yes, heavenly Father."

Whose hands was I holding? Were they the hands of the Father for them to be so big? Were they the hands of Jesus or of angels? Was I actually praying to God *while* holding His hands?" All these questions raced through my mind.

As I began to end the prayer, I gradually felt both women hands shrink back to normal, petite sizes.

That Rainbow

Debra H.
Middletown, CT

There was a woman from a church that I previously attended who had an outpatient procedure done and needed a ride back home from the outpatient center, so I volunteered. When I picked the woman up, she was a bit fearful of what was going on with her current health situation. I tried giving her words of encouragement, and during the conversation, we proceeded to talk on and on about the Lord.

While we were talking about Jesus and His goodness, I noticed an odd, bright, vertical rainbow beaming through the sky. I asked the woman if she saw it too, and she said she did. As we kept our eyes on it, we noticed the rainbow was moving. It was literally *moving*!

Not only was it moving, but it was headed in our direction, aiming straight for us!

The rainbow drew closer and closer until it smacked into my windshield. It was without a doubt supernatural! The very second it hit the windshield, we instantaneously started to scream and praise God at the same time. We couldn't stop praising because the moment the rainbow hit, the Holy Spirit fell on us and we *literally* couldn't stop praising Him.

This rainbow remained on my windshield for the duration of the trip, all the way up until I dropped the woman off at her home. This was truly a divine phenomenon!

"I set My rainbow in the cloud, and it shall be for the sign of the covenant between Me and the earth." –Genesis 9:13

6

I Saw God Last Night

THERE CAME A TIME WHEN I began surrounding myself with people who sincerely had a zeal for the Lord. Sometimes we would get together and watch videos of people sharing experiences with the Lord that fell far outside of our "thought box." They testified about being healed from HIV/AIDS, cancer and terminal illnesses, limbs growing back to normal lengths, eyeballs growing back into empty sockets, being teleported from dangerous situations to safe locations—even people leaving their bodies and taking trips to Heaven and/or Hell. All this was *extremely* new to me, but I wanted to know more.

At this time in my life, I was learning to keep God out of the box our society tends to put Him in. The "God doesn't do *that*" and "but that's impossible, things like that just don't happen" logics were long behind me and had fallen off a deep, long, not worthy-of-remembering cliff. I had realized that our concept of God goes far beyond logical thinking and not even the most brilliant intellectual could come close to understanding God's wonders (never forgetting that He made you, so guess whose brain is bigger?) God does what He wants (Philippians 2:13) and that's nothing we should be fearful of. All good things come from Him (James 1:17); All bad things come from Satan. We sometimes mix up the two, but when you meditate on God and His word, He will begin to reveal things to you.

The time came when I began to open myself up to the Lord and continually remind Him (not that He needs reminding) to use me as a vessel to do His will. I yearned for God to do something supernatural with me like all the testimonies I had heard time and time again, but nothing happened.

As I began to hear more and more testimonies of people going to Heaven or being visited by angels, I noticed that they were primarily men. I seriously began to believe within my heart that God was indeed a respecter of persons even though He says in His word that He isn't (Acts 10:34). It was during that time that God let me know through the supernatural that He had heard my prayers, knew my heart and thoughts, that He cared, and more so, that He is not a liar.

One night, in February 2010, my husband tucked our children into bed, we said our prayers and went to bed, just like every other night. At around three o'clock in the morning, I suddenly felt my spirit literally sit up *out* of my body! Immediately, I knew I was having what is known as an out-of-body experience. It was an unearthly knowing that is difficult to describe. The best way I can explain it is that my spirit literally separated from my body, as if I was going through an extremely narrow, skin deep sheet of air. I saw my body, but it was not *me*. For the first time, I saw my body for what it truly was—a shell—not a person, but the shell of a person...*my* person. I was still Jennifer and it amazed me. It wasn't dreamy at all.

I felt exactly the way I did when I was *in* my body. I could see, hear and feel, as if everything was still the same, except I was *out* of my body, instead of in.

While still in a sitting position on my bed (out of my body), I felt a special feeling inside *and* all around me. My spirit was alive! It was the best feeling I've had in my entire life! I've never used drugs or taken anything that would alter my sense of reality (except the time when the anesthesiologist gave me sedatives when I had my gallbladder removed in 2006 and I woke up loving everybody). This feeling was something that no drug or alcohol could ever come close to. It would be weeks before I'd realize that the indescribable feeling I had was the actual presence of the Lord and His presence was that of Love. Thus says the scripture, "To be absent from the body, and to be present with the Lord" (2 Corinthians 5:8).

As my euphoric state settled within me, I became fearful (since I was still fully conscious), then I began to reason with God, pleading, "Jesus, if You're going to show me Heaven or something, that's fine, but if You're going to *keep* me there, then please don't. I have a family with two children who need me." I began to reason and compromise with the Lord. I was trying to control the situation and not allow Him to take the lead. Like the gentleman that He is, instead of forcing me to go forward and do what *He* wanted, He rather gently laid me back down into my body.

The very second I was placed back into my body, I shot up out of bed and ran to the bathroom! "Am I going to die? If I lie back down will this happen again? Will God take me for good?" These were the questions circling in my head as I paced the bathroom floor. Making sure both toilet seat lids were down, I sat down, placed my head inside my hands and prayed. Still a little shaken up after 20 minutes in the bathroom, I grew tired and headed back to bed.

As I climbed into bed and wrapped the sheets around me, for the life of me I couldn't close my eyes out of apprehension that the same phenomenon would recur. I lay in bed badly wanting to sleep but my eyes were frozen wide open. I felt the air on my eyes as I strained to keep them open, then I whispered, "Jesus, please help me to sleep." Then next thing I knew, I was in an open vision!

I found myself in a bright white room. Standing before me was Jesus Christ smiling at me from a distance. He stood behind a beautiful, Louis XV chaise lounge rimmed in the finest gold with the most vibrant, peach-colored roses, hand-woven onto a cream-colored fabric with accents of threaded gold. It was the most beautiful piece of furniture I had ever seen.

He placed His hands on the top rim of the furniture, one hand on the right and the other on the left. Instead of being physically drawn to Jesus Himself, I was being drawn to the chaise lounge, gliding closer and closer. I sat down, leaned fully on my right side, lifted both my legs up onto the chaise, put my hands underneath the right side of my cheek (as if in a praying position) and rested my head. The second I laid down my head, I physically felt my eyes close in the natural realm.

When I awoke the next morning, I wanted to tell Ed, but for some reason I couldn't. I'm not sure if it was because of some residual shock or if the Lord wanted me to withhold it until the appropriate time. When night fell, I was able to let go of my reservations and tell my husband what happened the previous night.

"Babe, I sat up out of my body and I saw God last night!" I told him everything. The only thing I remember Ed saying after I was through was, "Wow!"

From the moment I finished telling my husband about the experience, the enemy immediately went to work on my mind. "Jesus was so disappointed in you. You didn't do what He wanted you to. You missed it. He's ashamed of you." Then I remembered the Bible calling Satan the "Prince of the Power of the Air" (Ephesians 2:2) and the "Accuser of the Brethren" (Revelation 12:10). Once I spoke it, the enemy knew, and now that he knew, he became my accuser, and I believed it.

Two or three days after my out of body experience and seeing Jesus, I was still full of guilt because of what the enemy was feeding me. So I did what I should have done in the first place: I prayed. I asked God if He was really disappointed and ashamed of me because I started compromising with Him.

He answered, "Remember the look on My face when you came to get rest? Did I *not* welcome you? Did I *not* look happy to see you? Did I *not* give you rest?"

From then on, my doubts were put to rest. I saw how much Jesus loved me. It didn't bother Him that I didn't go the next step (if there was one); I just remembered the way He looked at me. That Man loved me!

Three years later, I thought about what happened the night I saw Jesus standing behind that chaise lounge in my vision and wondered, "Why was I physically drawn to the chaise rather than Jesus Himself?" Just as I finished my thought, He spoke to my heart and said, "*I* am the Giver of Rest." I recalled the scripture from Matthew 11:28 that said, "Come to Me, all who are weary and heavy-laden, and I will give you rest." Jesus answered me, knowing my thoughts afar off (Psalm 139:2).

Over time, I began sharing my testimony and the response was shocking. Non-Christians were amazed and fascinated, wanting to know Who this "Jesus" was. Most of the time, they chose to give their life to the Lord.

One day, my husband and I sat down to have a conversation with two women of our family about the Lord, neither of whom was born-again. As we talked, Ed asked me to share my testimony with them. As I did, both women simultaneously began to grasp their arms and chests, asking, "What is *that*?"

One of them said, "I feel something good on me but I don't know what it is." The other agreed, adding, "Yeah, and I have chills going all through my body." I explained that what they were experiencing was the Holy Spirit manifesting Himself.

You see, the Holy Spirit (God) is everywhere, but He doesn't manifest everywhere. Many times He must be stirred up. God loves it when you continually talk about Him and when you worship Him. When you do, it's as if Heaven opens up above you and its remnants come pouring out into the atmosphere.

As we parted ways, one of the women was inspired to drive to the nearest Border's bookstore at around 9 o'clock at night, purchased her first Bible and give her life to the Lord! This has been the usual outcome when I tell non-believers my testimony.

So many people have no idea how extremely important it is to share your testimony, whatever it may be. It may be how God delivered you from drugs, alcohol, pornography, sexual confusion, stealing, depression, disease, gossip, etc. If you withhold your testimony and keep it only for yourself, ask yourself, "Whose life could

I SAW GOD LAST NIGHT

you have *eternally* saved if only they knew that only God could deliver them from the same mess you were told you could never be delivered from?" Don't hoard your testimony. Your testimony is *never* meant for only you.

Even more shocking than those conversion experiences were, when I told *Christians* my testimony, they'd look at me like I had four nostrils and a Cyclops eye! I even had one person very close to me, who was a minister for over 30 years, laugh in my face. That was not the reaction I expected at all. The worst responders were people ranked high in the ministry. The majority of them doubted every word I said and blew me off.

Honestly, I was disappointed in them—not because they didn't believe me (because I'm not what's important here), but because it was as if they wholeheartedly didn't believe that God worked in the supernatural other than healing the sick. Did they not believe John's testimony in Revelation 4:2 when he was taken up in the spirit into the Throne Room of God, or Paul in 2 Corinthians 12:1-3, when he says he was taken up into the third Heaven (actual Heaven) and whether still in the body or out he did not know? God didn't stop with the Bible! He didn't say, "Hey, I'll just start slacking off until the Rapture." No! He is still

100 percent active in our lives and performs the same miracles that we read about in the Bible.

An Appointment with Jesus

Gloria N.
Waterbury, CT

I was sleeping, and then all of a sudden, I (my spirit) left my body. When I turned myself around, I saw myself sleeping. While I was watching myself sleep, I heard a knock at the door. When I opened the door to see who it was, there stood two, huge, 8 foot tall angels dressed in all white! One had brown hair and the other one had golden blonde.

The angels smiled at me and said, "Hello, we've come for you because He is waiting for you." I turned to look at my sleeping body but it seemed as if I had passed away. I sort of felt sad because of my children, but a big part of me was as happy as a little child.

"Okay, let's go," I finally told them. As I stepped one foot out of the door, I immediately found myself in outer space! I was freaking out!

I looked at the angels and asked, "Don't you know that we will fall?"

Both angels looked at each other, smiled, looked back at me, then replied, 'Don't worry, we will be fine."

"Are you sure? 'Cause we are gonna fall!"

"I'm sure," one angel assured me.

From then on, we continued to walk, and as I looked around, I saw all of the stars, planets and galaxies. It was amazing! But still, I had the fear of falling. When I looked down, I noticed outer space beneath my feet. It was then that I realized that I was dressed in white with golden sandals.

When I set my eyes back on the angels, they said, "We stop here, but *you* must continue because He is waiting for you."

"What?" I blurted out in disbelief. "You want me to walk this alone...with no one?"

"You'll be fine. Go, because He is waiting for you," they encouraged me.

I said, "Okay," then walked on cautiously.

As I continued gazing around, I couldn't help but notice how beautiful and amazing everything was. Then all of a sudden, my eyes stopped at a man dressed in a garment with dark brown, medium length hair. He had His hands behind His back, pacing back and forth as if He was waiting for someone. As I drew steadily nearer to Him, I said, "Jesus?"

He turned around with a huge smile on His face and replied, "Daughter!"

I ran towards Him, and when I did, He quickly opened up His arms and embraced me. I fell into His arms. My fear of falling had become obsolete. I hugged Jesus so tight and I didn't want to let Him go. I looked up at His face and asked, "Did I die? Did You send for me already?"

He smiled and answered, "No, you did not die, but I *did* send for you because I wanted to talk to you." As we started to walk, He proceeded, "You see all this? It's all yours!"

"Really? Wow!" I gasped. I felt like the luckiest person ever!

"But I need you to do Me a favor. I need you to tell My people that the coming of the Lord is near. Many are still lost and My Father wants Me to go and pick up the church."

"Okay," I accepted, "but I don't want to go back. I want to stay here with You. I don't want to go back, *please*."

Jesus smiled, "You *have* to. It isn't your time yet, but I still need you to know that you *have* to alert the church. Many people think that my coming will take place a thousand years from now, but if *only* they knew I'm coming quickly. That's why I need you to alert them. There's no more time to lose."

"Alright, Jesus," I complied, "I will alert them."

My heart was sad because I didn't want to go back. I put my head down, and just as I was about to turn away, Jesus touched my chin, prompting me to look back up at Him.

"But get ready," He added, "because I'm coming for you." Jesus gave me that huge smile again and reminded me once more, "Go on and alert them. I *am* coming soon!"

I promised Him I would, and then gave Him a big hug and kiss on the cheek.

"You must go now because your family is waiting for you." He assured me.

I held His hand but didn't want to let it go, yet I knew I had to. As I walked away, I turned around to get one last glimpse of Him, but all I saw was *Him* turn around, shake His clothes, then an oval hole appeared. In it shone lots of light and clouds inside. Once He stepped into the oval hole, it closed up and disappeared.

I quickly turned to head back towards the area where the angels had last left me, and lo and behold, they were still there waiting for me. The two angels asked, "Are you ready?"

"Yes," I answered, "I was bummed because I didn't want to come back."

They looked at each other, smiled, then looked back at me and said, "I guess it isn't your time yet. Soon, though. Don't worry."

Once we arrived at the door where we entered, one of the angels said to me, "We're here now. Remember to say everything that He told you to say."

"I will," I promised.

I woke up and was back in my body.

"And behold, I am coming quickly, and My reward is with Me, to give to everyone according to his work. I am the Alpha and the Omega, the Beginning and the End, the First and the Last."
— Revelation 22:12-13

7

Crucifixion Profile

AS A CHILD AND even in my early adult years, I always wanted to go back in time and experience what it must have been like to live in Biblical times, just to view the lifestyle of the people, listen to the way they spoke and see the way they dressed. Many times I would pray and ask God for this experience in a dream. I would go to bed excited, thinking that when I'd go to sleep, I'd "awake" in the days of the Gospels, walk down the cobblestone roads of Jerusalem, gawk at the architecture, explore the cities and converse with the people. But each morning I'd wake up disappointed because instead I'd end up dreaming about an annoying hangnail or some other nonsense.

On Nov. 9, 2011, God finally answered my prayers, but *His* way. I was sitting on the sofa mid-afternoon, gazing out the window. Ed had just walked out the house to drag the trashcan to the curb of our driveway for garbage pickup the following day. The very instant he shut the door, I was taken into a vision where all I could see was a headshot or profile of Jesus Christ of Nazareth dying on a cross.

ISAW GOD LAST NIGHT

His head was tilted to the left, a crown of thorns was pressed into His head (John 19:2), and scarlet red blood glazed his entire face. There was an odd, disturbing sort of glistening darkness that bordered His sideburns down to His chin, then I realized that was where His beard once was before they ripped it from His face (Isaiah 50:6). One of the things that I noticed immediately was that there was blood all over the whites of His eyes, which were half open. There was so much blood that His hair was soaked and clotted in it.

The movie, *Passion of the Christ,* had *nothing* on what I was witnessing. This was suffering to the highest degree, and this was real. I was seeing Jesus in agony, becoming sin, dying a gruesome and inhumane death by the worst form of execution of the ancient world—crucifixion. And to think, He was doing this all for us (the people of this world) so that we wouldn't have to face eternal separation from Him as long as we believe that He did *this* for us and that He is Lord and resurrected!

There was another key factor in the vision: it was dark, I mean *really* dark, but I could still see His face and the blood glistening off of it. For some reason (probably because I wasn't reading my Bible like I should have at the time), I thought that the entire earth went dark the *moment* that Jesus died. When the vision ended, I couldn't make sense of why I saw Jesus still alive on the cross while it was dark. I knew the vision was directly from God and that God is never wrong. I just needed some clarity, so I opened my Bible and read for myself:

"It was now about the sixth hour (midday), and darkness enveloped the whole land and earth until the ninth hour (about three o'clock in the afternoon.). And the sun was darkened, and the veil of the temple was rent in the midst. And when Jesus had cried with a loud voice, He said, 'Father, into Thy hands I commend My spirit': and having said thus, He gave up the ghost" (Luke 23: 44-46).

Jesus *was* still alive when the earth went dark! Like I said, God is never wrong. One thing that I've come to realize about the Lord is that He will always give you confirmation, which proves the scripture, *"God has spoken once, twice I have heard this" (Psalm 62:11).*

For many months I questioned why the Lord revealed this, because to be honest, it startled me! The vision was graphic and the details were intense, definitely not like any image or painting I had ever seen of the Crucifixion. Seeing something like that is pretty hard to get out of your head, but in this case, I don't think I was supposed to.

I continued to ask God, "Why?" Why would He allow me to see this? Don't get me wrong, it was magnificent, but I just know that everything that God reveals to us has meaning.

By the early summer of 2013, I was *still* asking "why?", but by then I realized something: Every time I would ask Him, I'd inwardly answer my own question, blocking the door for the Lord to respond for Himself. I was getting in the way, again.

I began reading the last book of the four Gospels, St. John. As I began to read, I decided to chew on every word of it. I started to notice things about Jesus that I never had before. For one, everything He said was extremely bold and fearless, not soft and wimpy like depicted in films. I realized that He never sugar-coated *anything* or reworded things so that people wouldn't be offended. You could tell that Jesus instinctively knew what the people needed to hear and it wasn't a watered-down Gospel. This is only *one* of the reasons why everyone was so fascinated by Him when He spoke...even the Pharisees (John 7:26).

The second thing I learned was that He was emotional, not in a weak way by any means, but Jesus was thoughtful and truly loved the people. For instance, when He saw His friend Mary and the Jews weeping for Lazarus who had been dead for four days, scripture says Jesus groaned in the spirit and was troubled (His heart was hurting) and then it goes on to say, *"Jesus wept" (John 11:35).*

Jesus didn't cry because Lazarus had died. Days before, He told His disciples that He wasn't going to heal Lazarus because he had already died, then prophesied that He would *awaken* him (John 11:11-15). Jesus, knowing Lazarus was currently in paradise (Abraham's Bosom), and knowing that He would resurrect him, had nothing to cry over when it came to Lazarus himself.

Jesus cried because the people were hurting. He hated seeing them so deeply bereaved. That's how Jesus is: When we're hurting, He hurts, too. That's love.

I was finally able to put that controlling aspect of my free will aside long enough to hear Him answer my "Why?" His answer was what I had assumed all along. I guess I just needed His confirmation.

Jesus said, "I allowed you to see Me suffering on the cross so that you may see how much I truly love you. I did it all for you." He died for all mankind so we wouldn't have to be eternally separated from Him.

Life without Jesus is no laughing matter. The Bible says that all good things come from God and all good things are indeed a gift from above (James 1:17). Eternal life without Him would be absolutely no love, no rest, no mercy, no peace, no security, no safety, no laughter, no hope, no fellowship, and on and on.

The Crucifixion of Jesus Christ was one like no other in so many aspects. When I was a freshman in high school—when you could talk about Jesus in schools without risking a suspension—a fellow classmate once disagreed when I mentioned that Jesus is God.

The girl asked, "If Jesus was God, how come He died so fast on the cross? If He was God, He wouldn't have died so fast."

I explained to her that *because* He's God, He died so fast, and here's why: the moment every prophecy of old was fulfilled of His Crucifixion, and after His (earthly) mission was complete, there was no more reason for Him to stay hanging there alive. Jesus said it Himself: "It is finished" (John 19:30). His mission was completed. Scripture goes on to say that He "gave up the ghost," which is His spirit (Matthew 27:50). And because Jesus is God

(John 1:1-4, 14), no one can take His life from Him, He had to lay it down Himself, and *that* He did (John 10:18).

On the Cross

Buddy B.
Crestview, KY

While taking a shower, I was thinking about the Lord. The moment I closed my eyes, I saw countless angels facing Jesus. They were all standing at attention, as if they were ready and waiting for something. As they were facing Jesus, the Lord was full of a bright light surrounding Him, and I asked Him, "What is this?"

Jesus answered, "It's time!"

Then the vision changed, and I saw Jesus hanging on the cross. He was moving very little, I believe because of the pain. I could see how much pain He was in and I saw how badly He was beaten; it was worse than any movie or anything anyone could ever have come up with or even imagine. Nothing, I believe, can ever actually show how much Jesus really suffered for us. I couldn't get over what I was seeing—how much Jesus suffered.

The moment I opened my eyes, I was in shock. This vision really made me think and gripped my attention.

"So then Pilate took Jesus and scourged Him. And the soldiers twisted a crown of thorns and put it on His head, and they put on Him a purple robe. Then they said, "Hail, King of the Jews!" And they struck Him with their hands. Then he delivered Him to them to be crucified. So they took Jesus and led Him away. And He, bearing His cross, went out to a place called the Place of a Skull, which is called in Hebrew, Golgotha, where they crucified Him, and two others with Him, one on either side, and Jesus in the center. Now Pilate wrote a title and put it on the cross. And the writing was:

JESUS OF NAZARETH, THE KING OF THE JEWS.

-John 19:1-3, 16-19

8

Not from This Dimension

IF YOU ASK AND allow Him, God will show you things not of this world, things not of this dimension. If you sincerely give Him your life, your full trust and completely surrender, He will reveal things to you beyond your wildest imagination (Jeremiah 33:3).

Back on February 20, 2012, I woke up in the middle of the night (probably to turn over), and what I saw was so stunning and interesting that I didn't tell anyone for a good year in fear that no one would believe me.

I felt the Holy Spirit come upon me and my eyes not only became physically open, but also spiritually open. Stretching from the surface of my bed to beyond the ceiling (the ceiling had disappeared), was a glowing ladder made of pure crystal that stood before me. It was clear and sparkly. Light radiated all around it. Toward the top, the ladder cut through clouds that formed a circular entrance into Heaven. Heaven didn't seem so far away.

Strangely, that wasn't the part I was afraid people wouldn't believe. I thought they wouldn't believe the fact that along the base of the ladder fluttered the most beautiful, radiant, gleaming butterflies I had ever seen in my entire life. Like I said earlier, I'm not much of an animal/insect person, but I was in complete awe of them and felt like a little girl who had just seen butterflies for the very first time. They looked "fairytale-like," but this wasn't a fairy tale. Everything was *really* there.

Not only had the beauty of Heaven come to Earth, I wholeheartedly believe this was a heavenly portal, much like the ladder Jacob saw coming from the portal of Heaven (Genesis 28:12).

There was a similar occurrence two years later when I was laying in bed listening to Pandora radio on my iPod. All of a sudden, I saw this huge, golden, ancient staircase. One could tell that it was a staircase frequently used for thousands of years. It ran through outer space, speckled with it's stars and galaxies. At the very top of the stairwell was an open door to Heaven and in the doorway stood Jesus. He was just looking at me as if He had been watching me for a while. I could see people walking behind Him up there, going about their day. Heaven looked busy but in a serene way.

Immediately when the vision was over, the song on the radio changed to "Come Up Here", sung by Jason

Upton. I was in complete shock when I heard the lyrics. It spoke of a person looking up and seeing the doorway to Heaven standing wide open. Then the Lord called this person His "beloved" and invited them to come up there.

My jaw dropped and stayed that way for a good minute or so. I was in awe of my vision's confirmation!

I've often wondered why so many of these heavenly experiences occurred in my bedroom, and the best explanation I've come up with is: besides my living room, that's one of the places I spend most of my time communing with God.

One experience I'm about to share with you happened either through a dream or an open vision, I'm not sure of which:

While standing in my bedroom, I felt like something was amiss, like my life was out of control. As I left my bedroom, there stood two beautiful angels, one each on my top two stairs. I had never seen an angel before, let alone *two*! These particular angels didn't have wings, nor were they giant. Their perfection was out of this world (pun intended). They had long, blonde, combed back hair and not a single hair out of place. Even the best hair stylist couldn't mimic their impeccable locks; no hairspray or gel could do the trick, either.

107

Their skin was white but they were not of any one race or nationality. Their noses were pointy and their entire being glowed radiantly in light. These angels stood at attention as if they were on assignment. Immediately I knew...Jesus was coming! The angels were on guard because their King, *our* King, was entering the atmosphere.

Ashamed of where my life stood at that current time (in the dream or vision), I ran and hid. Who did I think I was fooling? You can't run from God! Jonah was the perfect example of that (Jonah 1:1-17). I scurried to my children's room, pulling the door closed behind me. There I was in a tiny, dim, triangular corner...hiding from *Jesus*!

Suddenly, the brightest light I had ever seen filled the room and I knew it was *Him!* Jesus was coming for me. He pulled the door open and all I could make out was a figure made of pure light. He was glorious! I couldn't make out His face or any other detail—He was too bright, but not to the point where it hurt my eyes. It was as if I was made to look at Him.

Still ashamed of myself, I shrugged down a little as I saw Jesus' hand of light reach for me and touch my right shoulder. The moment He touched me, I was immediately filled with His love and my shame completely vanished. I was powerless. He had me. Just by His one touch, I was changed. He had total control and it was "His way or His way"; the highway wasn't even an option. His way was the *only* way; the perfect way.

It amazed me because I felt Jesus touch me...*literally*! When I sat up (or woke up) out of bed, I was saturated and filled with the Holy Spirit for the entire rest of the day.

***

There are times when I wake up in the middle of the night—usually around 3 a.m., and feel the raw, manifested, literal presence of the Almighty God. When it happens, I'm often consumed with the fear of God. Someone once asked me, "If God knows you're going to be scared, then why does He come to you?" I explained to them that it's not that He's scary or even that I'm all that afraid; I feel the fear of God in me because when He's present, His power is made perfectly clear. When He's manifested in your presence in this way, you *know* and realize that He has your life in His hands and that *He* has the power to sustain or take your life. You have the fearsome knowledge that He really *does* rule this universe and beyond. When He is manifested, the knowledge of His greatness is so strong that you feel it in your bones.

***

Through dreams and visions, God has shown me many different heavenly things that I have *never* seen on earth. I've seen unique-looking flowers with a distinct depth of color and glisten to them. He's also shown me small bits of the perfections of heavenly nature as well.

Jesus has appeared to me four times in very different ways so far in my life, all before the age of 30, and it has been entirely for His purpose for my life and for others. This is why it really disappoints me when I hear ministers shutting people down who come to them testifying that Jesus appeared to them. These ministers will sometimes say, "I don't believe that! Jesus is sitting at the right hand of the Father; therefore, Jesus couldn't have appeared to you." What a shame. It hurts my heart.

Yes, it's true that Jesus is sitting on the right hand of the Father, scripture says so (Romans 8:34), but I wonder if these ministers forget that Jesus appeared to Paul on the Road to Damascus *after* His heavenly ascension (Acts 26: 12, 15-16). Do they overlook the fact that Jesus

NOT FROM THIS DIMENSION

also appeared to John on the Isle of Patmos *after* His heavenly ascension (Revelation 1: 12-18)? Would they dare say this to prisoners of war who have testified of Jesus physically coming to them while imprisoned and Him giving them divine strength? Have they also forgotten that our almighty God is omnipresent and that He is not confined to one spot (Psalm 139:7-10, Matthew 28:20, 18:20, Acts 17:27)?

Jesus is not chained to a chair! He can be on the throne, while at your house and in China all at the same time because He's *God!* He is *not* limited, and we need to be careful in limited thinking when it comes to the King of Kings and Lord of Lords; the First and the Last; the Beginning and the End; the Bright and Morning Star; the I AM!

Jesus meant it when He said:

"Assuredly, I say to you, unless you are converted and become like children, you will by no means enter the Kingdom of Heaven." -Matthew 18:3

Adults must change their way of thinking. I don't know what happens to us when we get older, but it seems as if our hearts wax cold over the innocence inside of us

111

that's really not meant to go away. We stop believing in miracles and lose the "mountain moving faith" God has given each and every one of us (Matthew 17:20).

Not too long ago, I shared a song of angels singing by Elias Arguello with a group of children ages 5 to 14, and I was taken aback by their response. After hearing the song, almost every last child couldn't wait to tell me of their own supernatural experience with God, Heaven and/or angels. Each one couldn't wait to squeeze their story in.

It was *amazing* and I was amazed *by* them— children who knew what they experienced and had no doubt about it. One little girl's face lit up when she told me how she had a dream that God gave her a tour of Heaven. When she described it, it was in such great detail. She assured me that Heaven was fun. By what she described, it wasn't the boring misconception of people floating on clouds playing the harp or standing in one spot for all eternity singing songs. Yet, when another (Christian) adult walked into the room and heard the story, they blew it off!

⚹ We *must* start listening to and believing our children, especially when it comes to their experience with the Lord God.

When I was five or six years old, my father took the whole family to Sizzler Restaurant for dinner. I'll never forget how we sat at a table with a chandelier that had non-coated, clear light bulbs. I think that was the first time I had ever seen a light bulb without the white coating on the outside of it. I was mesmerized. I must have stared at that light for the entire first part of my meal, but when I took my eyes off of it, I began to see what appeared to be little, glowing, floating, long legged bugs.

I reacted like any other little girl would have, I started spazzing out!

"I see things floating around! They're on your head!" I yelled.

I assured people at the table, but nobody believed me—except for my father.

My dad said something in the lines of, "Jenny, I believe you. I know kids see things that adults sometimes don't. Don't worry, honey."

That did my heart good. There's nothing like having a parent who listens to you and believes in you.

Some 15 years later, I had to break it to my dad and tell him that I finally figured out it was actually the glowing filament (the coil looking thing inside a light bulb) that had been temporarily stamped on my vision that night as a child. But like the great dad that my father is, he wouldn't let that story go and still insists that I saw something supernatural that night (even though I didn't; gotta love him). He understood that God uses children in ways that He doesn't with adults because of their childlike faith.

My children have had dreams of Jesus appearing to them and can describe Him almost perfectly, from His hair, to His clothes, even His smile. They heavily emphasized how nice Jesus was, and guess what? *I believe them!*

We must get to the point where we don't just kill, but annihilate our doubt so faith can take residence in our hearts and minds. It is our Christian obligation to give God the opportunity to open our eyes to His supernatural and miraculous wonders.

I Went to Heaven, Mommy: A Testimony of Juan Hugo

Adele B., Mother of Juan Hugo
Port Elizabeth, South Africa

We would like to bear witness to God's love, mercy and blessings upon our lives. My husband, Hugo, and I have two beautiful children—a nine year old daughter and seven year old son. When I was expecting my daughter, the Lord gave me Psalm 23, that God will protect her, and our boy, Psalm 27.

My daughter, Kirsten (means "follower of Christ"), was born healthy with no complications.

A year and a half later, our son, Juan Hugo (Juan is derived from John and means "gift from God"), was born three weeks early with the umbilical cord wrapped twice around his neck. We got a big fright when we saw him for the first time because he was blue-purple, almost black, as the umbilical cord strangled him. We realized that if he was not born on that day he would not have survived. The day after his birth, when the nurses were supposed to bring him to be fed, they never came. I was informed that our boy had stopped breathing twice. But the Lord has been so wonderful and all the glory to God for saving our beautiful son in those first days. Many people prayed for him and prophesied that he would one day work for the Lord.

October 2010—When Hugo was three years old, we found him standing on a wooden bench preaching. He shouted, "Do not run away! Listen to Jesus!" He often walked around the house worshipping and then just shouting, "Jesus! Jesus!"

One morning, he woke me up and told me he dreamt of purple and orange bees that were attacking him and that he was boxing them. While boxing the bees, their

wings fell off and Jesus helped him put the bees in a basket
that the Lord then threw into Hell. He described how the
big black gate of Hell opened and that the fire was very
high. He felt as if he was almost was going to fall into it,
but said he wasn't afraid. When asked what he had seen, he
said that he saw people. Some said, "I believe Jesus arose,"
and others said, "Give me some water. Give me some
water."

He added that he saw a lot of smoke and heard a
noise that he couldn't describe.

After that, Jesus took him and showed him Heaven.
He said Jesus was wearing a gold belt and gold shiny
shoes—but the shoes look like boots. Jesus was also
wearing white pants with a blue shirt and Hugo said he had
the same clothes on.

In Heaven, he saw lions, elephants, giraffes and
rhinos, and mentioned the lions don't bite and also how he
touched the rhino's horn. Jesus showed him little lambs; he
held one and gave him milk.

Hugo said Jesus no longer had a crown of thorns,
rather He now has a brand new crown that he described
with white and red lights on it (rubies and diamonds that
shine). He said that Jesus took him to a river where they

caught a fish and Jesus cooked the fish for them. Jesus also gave him juice to drink that tasted just like watermelon, and that it was delicious.

Our son told us that he and Jesus played on the grass and expressed how excited he was about the beautiful flowers he saw, with colors of blue, yellow and pink that were *singing!* (The flowers singing can be confirmed by a number of other people who also had Heaven experiences.)

He said that Jesus told him, "Hugo, I'm going to show you your house now," and then gave him a book and told him that he needed to write down everything he saw. He spoke of the gold and shiny streets that were transparent like glass. His house had his name written on the door and was a double or triple story house, with a very big roof and lots of stairs.

Hugo spoke of the beautiful furniture, including a particular chair or stool that embraced you as you were sitting in it, but no TV. He saw a round tub with beautiful gold taps. His bed and cupboard were full of toys and there was something that he liked a lot but we couldn't work out exactly what it was. There was also a green tractor with a purple roof.

He also spoke of the fruit that he ate there and told us of this big angel that he saw, and that Jesus sent this angel (Michael) to help someone on earth.

Hugo saw many famous people from the Bible, including: Father Abraham, who had welcomed him as he came into Heaven, and also David (his hero), along with many other people and children. He said that David asked him, "What are you doing here already?"

While telling us about Heaven, Hugo asked my mother about her parents who had passed away. He said that he saw my mother's father and told her that he was very kind and handsome. Little Hugo also saw my husband's grandparents. When my mother asked him how old her father was, as old as their mid 50's or as old as their 30's, he answered, "As old as Daddy and Mommy—30s."

Next, Jesus showed him His throne. He said the throne was beautiful and was made out of wood and gold and that there were many people praising and singing to the Most High God. Everybody was on their knees with their heads bowed down. He saw a very bright light coming from the Throne of God and many angels as well.

An angel took him to God and He greeted Hugo with a, "Hello".

He said that God had told him that He can see that his family loves Him very much and that we are nearly there.

Hugo tells of the tunnel that they came through and the gate they went through into Heaven. He speaks of clouds that he touched, that they felt like nothing. Also, of many roads and that Jesus said that one should make sure that you choose the right path (Matthew 7:13-14).

We recognize the purity of this child and the importance and urgency of this message. Jesus showed him all of these things and instructed him to go and tell the people that Heaven and Hell is a reality.

Hugo said that God wanted him to write it down (at 3 years old he could not yet write) so we wrote this testimony from his description, and we believe God will mark it in his heart so that he will remember it always.

These encounters are an urgent call to get our lives straightened out, and to get excited and earnestly desire the soon coming of the Lord. MARANATHA, COME JESUS COME!

Talking to Jesus

Sara D., Mother of Josiah, 2 years old
Meriden, CT

One afternoon, my husband and I took our two little boys to their grandfather's house to visit. When we got to the house, the children took off playing. After we adults were finished talking amongst ourselves, we went off looking for them. We found our oldest son, but had trouble locating our youngest, who was two years old at the time. As we searched the house, we finally heard his voice trailing down the hall; he was talking to Someone. When we finally found him, he was in his grandfather's bedroom still chatting away—but there was no one else in the room with him. We asked him, "Josiah, who are you talking to?"

"Jesus", he answered.

"Jesus?" I replied in shock.

"Yeah, Jesus is right there on the bed. He's smiling at me."

Then Josiah began waving at Him, but *we* couldn't see anything. To our surprise, he kept on with their conversation while we were still with him in the room.

✳ *"Then they also brought infants to Him that He might touch them; but when the disciples saw it, they rebuked them. But Jesus called them to Him and said, "Let the little children come to Me, and do not forbid them; for of such is the kingdom of God. Assuredly, I say to you, whoever does not receive the kingdom of God as a little child will by no means enter it."*

–Luke18:15-17

9

The Holy Spirit

MY FRIEND, ESTER, INTRODUCED me to spontaneous worship music a few years back, although at first I thought it was rather strange. It wasn't the type of Christian or Gospel music I was used to; there was no particular order of these songs or rhythmic patterns, the songs simply poured from the heart.

One morning, I asked Esther to stop by and help me clean out my basement. She was willing and asked if she should bring some music. That caught me off guard because I usually don't clean with music; for me, silence makes me work quicker. So I asked her what kind of music she was hoping to bring and she said, "Worship music."

I figured, "Why not?" It wouldn't hurt to try something new.

That spring afternoon, Esther pulled up in my driveway in her red Toyota Camry, walked her two children into the house to play with my daughters and met me in the kitchen. As we began to make small talk, she realized she'd forgotten the music in the car, so she went back out to get it.

In the meantime, I got a rag, stood between the stove and kitchen island, and began wiping down the island counter. As I continued to wipe, I completely forgot that Esther had left the house. Laser-focused on the countertop, I began to hear a faint melody coming from outside that got louder by the second. As the sound of the music drew closer, I was getting a quickening in my spirit! I *knew* what was happening! I had felt this before, but never at home— *never in my own kitchen!* The Holy Spirit was present, at work, and literally manifesting Himself in my house! My knees became weak and tingly. My body got heavier because my legs were giving way. God was there and I couldn't withstand His glory!

My mind started to race. I was excited for God's presence. I had experienced Him so many other times before, but every time He shows up, it's always like the very first time all over again.

As my fingertips gripped the top of the island, my body slouched over the edge to keep myself standing. I looked to the right to see Esther nonchalantly walking up the deck stairs towards the kitchen holding her iPhone, which was playing the music I was hearing.

She slid open the screen door slider and stepped inside.

"What are you doing?" I breathed to her as my entire body began to lose strength, including my voice.

"What?" she said confused and still blasting the music on her phone.

"I can't stand, turn it off. Turn it off," I urged, although I was sort of reluctant to have her turn it off because I knew the Lord was still at work.

Esther looked at me like I was crazy and started to chuckle as if thinking, "What on earth is wrong with you?" I don't think she was able to make out what I was saying because of the low tone in my voice.

Still a bit confused, she asked again, "What?"

"Turn it off!" I squealed. By this point I was seconds away from falling to the ground.

"Oh. Okay," Esther said, hitting the pause icon on her phone.

She began to chuckle as my strength returned.

"What was wrong with you?"

"You didn't feel that?" I asked.

"Feel what?"

"You didn't *feel* that?" I asked again.

"Feel *what*?"

"The Holy Spirit! He was here and I couldn't stand up 'cause His glory was so strong. What song was that? What song were you playing?"

She told me it was a song by Eddie James called "Draw Nigh."

I smiled, "I think I like that song."

By this time, the children were playing all throughout the house. I walked over to the stairs, calling out to them to make sure they were alright. The very moment I turned to walk away from my staircase, the dream I had the previous night came back to my recollection. What I had just experienced in the kitchen, I dreamt the night before—down to every detail. The only difference was, in my dream, I literally ended up falling to the floor and began soaking in His love—what many would call as being "slain in the spirit." In my dream, I was in the same exact spot in the kitchen, between the island and the stove, slouching over an island counter and falling to the ground under the weight of God's presence.

When I look back at that moment, I realize that I should have let the Lord do what He wanted with me, instead of me trying to control the experience He was gifting me. I know this because I saw the outcome in the dream the night prior.

Esther and I made our way down to the basement. She rested her Bose speaker on a black little folding tray I had sitting adjacent to the stairs on the finished side of my basement. Fitting her iPhone on the speaker dock, she asked me to listen to a song called, "Mi Amor" by Elias Arguello.

"What do you think of this song?" she asked. "When this guy sings, he says angels sing with him, and this time an angel's voice was captured singing during a studio recording. Tell me what you think. Do you think this is really an angel?"

It was one of the most beautiful songs I had ever heard. Even though the song was sung in Spanish and I was unable to understand the words, it didn't matter; it was clearly a love song to Jesus.

It took a few minutes to get to the part of the angel singing. It sounded as if it had vocal cords made of oversized pipes—airy, strong, and yet beautiful.

"Yes, I believe this *is* an angel singing with him," I answered.

"Really? What makes you say that?" Esther asked.

It was then that I opened up to her about the first time I heard angels singing a few months prior:

I had dropped the kids off at school and when I got back home, for some reason, I decided to go back to bed. This was pretty unusual for me because when I get back up from a second round of sleep, I usually end up feeling sluggish and lazy, so I try to avoid doing so.

When I opened my eyes from about an hour long nap, I realized I had left the television on to TBN. Joyce Meyers was preaching at what looked like one of her conferences. I closed my eyes again to, as people say, "rest my eyes." Suddenly I began to faintly hear singing—it was a choir! My right eye partly opened, then the other. I stared at Joyce on the television screen and said to myself, "Joyce doesn't have choirs singing while she's speaking." Looking at the clock, it said it was a quarter to the hour. Again, I said to repeat, "She *definitely* doesn't have anyone singing in the middle of her sermons!"

Upon that realization, I threw the covers from off of me and jumped out of bed! Whatever was going on was very strange to me. I put my ear to the alarm clock to see if it was the radio. It wasn't. A church sat a block or two down the street and around the corner. I usually hear the bells ringing on the hour every day, so I figured maybe the sound could be coming from the church. I opened my window, shoved my ear to the screen—still nothing. The television was still on. Hmmm, maybe it *was* coming from Joyce Meyer's show. I pressed the power off button and…still singing!

"Could this be angels I'm hearing?" I asked myself with a little smirk on my face. After all, that would be pretty cool. It's not every day you hear angels when you wake up from your sleep, or if you do, you're *dead!* But I knew I was alive and there was a distinct possibility that I could have been hearing angels, nevertheless, I needed to be sure.

First, I wanted to make sure I wasn't just hearing things, so I stuck both fingers in my ears and there was silence. Great—it wasn't in my head! When I pulled my fingers out of my ears, I could hear the beautiful choir again. It was a tad bit louder and clearer this time, but I couldn't make out the lyrics. I walked out of my bedroom and into the upstairs hallway and *still* heard the singing.

From room to room upstairs, to room to room downstairs, the singing continued. No matter where I went, the sound of the choir stayed at the same volume—no closer, no further, just…there. If I were to pull back an invisible curtain that separated me from the supernatural realm, I could have possibly been looking right at them. The sound was beautiful—as if singing voices coming from large, crisp pipes that I'm unable to humanly describe.

I heard angels that day and I was glad I was able to give Esther an answer.

***

I'd often talk long distance with my cousin who isn't a Christian (she is of a different religion). We would talk about Jesus, the god she serves and the differences between the two. She was often curious about Jesus and why Christians believe the things we do. I'd tell her about miracles, the power that the name of Jesus holds and how He lives in each and every one of His children (those who are born again).

On a side note, I used to believe that everyone was God's child because the saying had become so cliché, even Gospel songs are written saying so, until my late grandmother's friend taught me otherwise. At first I thought she was talking crazy, but when someone mentions something so impactful, it seems to stick in the back of your mind. She'd say to me with such wisdom, "You know Jennifer, we are *not* all God's children. We're all His finest creation, but we are not all His children. You become His child once you give your life to Him and are born again, then you become a part of His family." It wasn't until I opened the Bible that I found this to be absolutely true (John 1:12-13, Roman 9:8, Galatians 3:26, 4:5-7).

One day, my cousin called me up sounding super excited. She told me that she and her children had just arrived back home from her neighbor's funeral, who happened to be a Christian, and that she had never been to a funeral like the one she went to that day.

"The people were so happy, Jennifer!" she gushed.

I explained to her, "That's what we call a Going Home Service. The people were happy because they know the woman went to Heaven. This is usually a celebration for us."

"Well, Jennifer, let me tell you: Me and my daughter was just sitting there, then all of a sudden, it felt like somethin' came inside of me. I jumped out my seat and started dancin'!" she said. "I couldn't control it! And you know what? It felt so good, Jennifer! I've never felt like that before. And my daughter...I looked next to me and there she was dancin' *too*! We both couldn't control ourselves. I don't know what was happening to me, but I loved it!"

Her tone suddenly became very serious, "You wanna know somethin'? I *never* once felt like that when I was in my religious outfit. I always felt down." Then her attitude switched back to being excited again, "But now that that happened to me, I'm just gonna let God do whatever He wants with me! Whatever He wants me to do, I'm gonna let Him do it!"

After she was done speaking, I explained to her that what she felt was the Holy Spirit. It filled my heart with such joy to hear her testimony—proving yet again that God is not a respecter of persons (Acts 10:34). My cousin was not a Christian and He still considered her.

He will go to extreme measures to help open our eyes to the truth of His existence and His love for us. God doesn't want to lose a single soul. Not one. I truly believe that the Lord will continue fighting for each and every one of us up until we take our last breath. He is a determined God!

Silhouette of Jesus

Debra H.
Middletown, CT

In 1999, my son passed away at the age of 21. During this time, I was feeling led to do something spectacular for the Lord because through it all, I still strongly desired to worship Him. So I decided to plan a fundraiser event for my church. After brainstorming on what type of fundraiser to do, I came to the conclusion that I wanted to do something "big" and book the famous, gospel pianist, Ben Tankard, for the event. The only problem was, I hadn't any money, but this didn't hinder me from trying. So I picked up the phone and dialed his 1-800 number expecting to reach his manager, but was totally surprised when Ben Tankard, himself, answered the phone! As I conversed with him and told him a bit about my church, he explained what he offered, when he was available, and what the booking cost would be.

When I hung up the phone, I was a bit discouraged because I had no clue where I would get the money from to make this fundraiser come to fruition; so I did what I knew best—I prayed. Immediately after I got done praying, Jesus said to me, "Ask your husband."

A few days later, my husband and I got together for lunch. By this time, I still hadn't mentioned the fundraiser to him. As we were chatting, out-of-the-blue, he asked me what project I was currently working on (as I am a coordinator). I told him about the huge fundraiser my heart was set on doing for the church and how I desired to incorporate Ben Tankard.

My husband asked me how much money I needed to reserve the artist. I told him the cost. He then looked into my eyes and promised, "Honey, I'll have the money to you by this Friday!"

I was shocked and amazed! After everything my husband and I were currently going through with the loss of our son, God was still proving Himself to be faithful.

The day finally came for the fundraiser which was hosted on the town green in Middletown, CT. The crowd was present, everything was running smoothly, and Tankard and his crew were on stage worshipping with songs and instruments. The music could be heard downtown for blocks away.

As I started worshipping God and thanking Him for always being there for me, I raised my eyes to the sky to thank Him even more, and then all of a sudden, my eyes were locked on a huge silhouette! It was Jesus continuously waiving His right hand across the sky over the crowd of people! It was so surreal! I had never seen anything like it before.

Shofar, Angels and a Visitation

Simone F.
Wichita, KS

I grew up in a home where good grades and good manners were always expected, but there was absolutely no Godly instruction and I virtually knew nothing about God, yet in my heart I knew He existed.

I was aware that there was a Heaven and Hell—so much that I even baptized myself in the bathtub with sprinkles of water when I was around four or five years old. My mother thought that was "cute", but I was terribly serious. I wanted to know God but didn't really have a clue where to begin. I felt the aversion from everyone in my family when I talked about God, which greatly confused and upset me.

One day, when I was about 7 or 8 years old, I saw a kind, black man named Lonnie walking up the steps to my parent's home. He worked for my dad pouring concrete. This man was different and I perceived in my spirit that Jesus Christ was with him. Jesus, the Son of God! I was amazed and instantly loved Lonnie. Years later, I would hear about his death in a house fire—about how he died trying to get his blind sister out of the house. This undoubtedly was the Godly nature that I knew a true Christian possessed.

When I went to the funeral with my dad, I cried for this man who I had never known personally, but yet who touched my heart so much. My dad mentioned that many times when the construction crew would eat lunch outside on a nice day, Lonnie would get out his Bible and preach the Word of God to the people.

I so craved for this God that finally, when I turned 15, I found the Lord and gave my life to Him. Instantly, I knew that I had been translated from spiritual darkness into spiritual light. It was so very profound and I knew that I had made an incredibly important, eternal decision that spring day. Finally, I felt alive! God began to put Christians in my path and He protected me from so many things. He kept showing Himself, but the most amazing thing as a baby Christian happened to me only months after my conversion:

I got up one beautiful, summer morning, and after I made my bed I was drawn to look out of my window. The cloudless sky was the bluest blue I had ever seen it. I was mesmerized by it! Suddenly, I heard it. I heard three blasts of a trumpet, but it didn't sound like a regular trumpet. I would later find out it was a shofar. I then heard the angels singing. To this day, I remember how beautiful and pure their voices were. I asked people what they thought this meant but no one could tell me. God then led me to read Psalm 47, which talks about the Lord being King of the Earth. I'd also wonder if the Rapture would happen in *my* lifetime. I didn't draw the correlation between the Feast of Trumpets and the Catching Away of the saints until much later, but it makes me think that perhaps God was giving me several messages with that experience. I see Biblical prophecy unfolding all around me and it is very possible that Jesus Christ could come and get His church at *any* time now.

In 1991, my mind became bombarded by many questions. I had so many that I can't even remember what they all were, but I do remember one of them: What happened once we died and leave our bodies? Do we fall asleep or do we go on, fully aware to our destination?

That spring, I remember going over to my parents' house to visit. I was in the foyer and my mind was still being bombarded by the Holy Spirit. I remember my dad wanted my husband to come out to the garage to look at something and my mother suggested that I look for a book for my daughter to read to her. They both went around the corner to her large master bedroom while I stood at the large bookcase wondering what book I could find.

Suddenly, a book literally "popped" out, landing on the wooden floor of the foyer. I picked it up and decided that I'd like to read it for myself. The thick, paperback book that is now out of print was called, *World Aflame*, by Billy Graham. Later, when I read through it, it answered every single question that was shelled up in my mind at the time. I knew that God was drawing me to become His disciple and leading me to start learning more about Him and His kingdom. I was excited and touched that God cared enough about me to *want* me to know more about Him.

In March of 1993, I would have a visitation from the Lord that lasted six months. I know it sounds strange, but God's ways are not our ways and this is how He dealt with me. I will always cherish how He came and made His abode with me. To describe that time would be to say that it was a private and holy time. It was a time where I saw God's beautiful heart and was anointed daily by His Holy Spirit. It was literally a rubbing of my forehead in a circular motion but soon after this, I could feel the anointing just billow around me like big, invisible sheets. I would be reading the Bible and in the spirit I would feel and hear the vibrations of His footsteps walking toward me. I felt spiritual warfare going on in my home quite often, feeling the angels battling things out with evil in the spiritual realm.

Last but not least, the very first time I heard the voice of God was when I was upset over the fact that some people were saying that Christians would have to go through the Tribulation. I anguished over this. So, finally one day, when I was speaking to God about this...He spoke back! I heard it very clearly in my spirit, and it was like someone had set headphones over my ears. He said, "THE BODY OF CHRIST SHALL NEVER BE IN TRAVAIL AGAIN." I later found scriptures that backed this up. After that, and to this day, I will no longer debate anyone on that subject. It was mind-boggling to think that God cared so much about me truly needing an answer, that He actually spoke to me, allowing me never to have to question it ever again.

"And there appeared an angel unto Him from Heaven, strengthening Him." -Luke 22:43

10

Know the Voice of God for Yourself

IT IS IMPERATIVE THAT you know the voice of God for *yourself*; otherwise, you can and will be fooled and lured into lies of the enemy (Satan).

Jesus said it Himself:

> *"My sheep hear My voice, and I know them, and they follow me." -John 10:27*

A person may ask, "How do I get to the point where I can distinguish the voice of God above all others?"

The truth is, it becomes quite simple when you daily devote your personal time to God by reading His Word, praying and meditating on Him. For me, every morning before I eat breakfast, watch TV, use the computer or spend time with my family, I dedicate the very first hour of my day to spending time with Jesus. I ask for discernment while chewing on a Bible chapter or two, and then I sit quietly in prayer and meditation.

Even though God speaks to you whenever He desires, the time you *choose* to spend with Him is more endearing. He delights in your willing company and begins to speak to your spirit and reveal things to you that no person, no matter how faithful, could ever reveal.

Most of the time we don't hear Him with our ears (although many people have heard the audible voice of God); we hear Him in our Spirit. If it were in our minds, it would just be our own thoughts or deception from the enemy, but God works bigger than that. He speaks to our inner man, our spirit and soul. Put plainly, if it's in your brain, it's not Him. When He speaks, if you're His child, you will know His voice.

✳ *"To him the doorkeeper opens, and the sheep hear his voice; and he calls his own sheep by name and leads them out. And when he brings out his own sheep, he goes before them; and the sheep follow him, for they know his voice. Yet they will by no means follow a stranger, but will flee from him, for they do not know the voice of strangers."*
-John 10:3-5

Because Scripture compares all of mankind to sheep who have gone astray (Isaiah 53:6) and sheep without a

146

shepherd (Matthew 9:36), before we give our life to Christ, we are lost and misled, following every "Tom, Dick, and Harry" around. But when Christ becomes our Shepherd and we His sheep, we become *His*, and His voice becomes distinct and familiar to us.

I'll never forget the time when the Lord sent me a dream about the daughter of a leader in a church. When I woke up from the dream, I was terrified; mainly because I didn't know how to interpret it and I saw the dream as being literal (by which most dreams aren't, but rather symbolic). All I knew to do was get on my knees and pray, so I did.

This was the dream:

I saw the mother, father and brother of a young lady who had just passed away a month before her wedding day. They were holding each other, weeping and mourning over her outside the church nursery.

I couldn't figure out the meaning of this dream for the life of me, until one day, out of the blue, the Lord just decided *then* was the best time to shed some light on it.

This was God's interpretation:

The young lady in the dream was not called to marry the man she was presently engaged to. The reason why the family was crying outside of the nursery was because if she were to go along with this marriage, the Lord would close up her womb—that was the death.

Finally, closure and peace came upon me, but at the same time, the interpretation seemed pretty blunt. But that's how God is—straightforward. Then I asked myself if God really closes wombs, and after reading Genesis 20:18 and 1 Samuel 1:6, it affirmed that He does.

I knew I had to tell the young lady and her parents about the dream along with the divine interpretation, but I was a bit nervous to say something so serious and direct. I didn't know the young lady except for saying "hi" a couple of times in passing and I had never once spoken to her fiancé. I knew very little about them.

Until then, I would pray for the Lord to give this young lady direction. It was a blessing and relief when I got word a week later that she had called off the wedding.

Although the wedding had already been called off, a friend advised me that I should still let the young lady know about the interpretation of the dream that God had

KNOW THE VOICE OF GOD FOR YOURSELF

given me, so I first arranged a quick sit-down meeting with her mother.

I told her the dream. As I got to the part where I told her that her daughter had died, she began to cry, which made me tear up a bit too, and then I proceeded until the end. Along with assuring her that the death in the dream wasn't physical, I gave her the (bold and blunt) divine interpretation given directly to me from God.

It was then that the woman attempted to correct me. She glanced up at the ceiling as if she were listening for something and responded, "I'm not saying you're wrong, but what *I'm* actually getting is that my daughter wouldn't have a passion for singing on the worship team anymore if she had married him (her ex-fiancé). *That's* what I'm getting what the dream meant."

I was dumbfounded and speechless. Usually when someone says, "I'm not saying you're wrong," what he or she is really saying is, "You're wrong!" But what was most important is that I *knew* without a shadow of a doubt what the Lord revealed to me, and it wasn't what this woman was telling me. Yet, because I knew God's voice and was able to distinctly recognize the voice of my heavenly Father, I stood firm. Of course, from a mother's standpoint, I can clearly understand why she'd rather it be something less severe and come up with a lighter interpretation.

Here's the "kicker": The mother decided it would be a good idea for me to tell the dream and interpretation to her daughter who was in a separate part of the church, and I agreed. When her daughter finally entered into the room and closed the door, I laid it all out for her just as I did for her mother, and her response was, "Wow!" She then looked to her mother and said, "That finally explains the dream I had last year when I saw myself singing on stage during praise and worship. While I was singing, I looked down and saw a huge, empty hole in my stomach!"

※ God will *always* give you confirmation of whatever He reveals to you, thus proves the scripture, "God has spoken once, twice have I heard this" (Psalm 62:11). No matter what any minister, priest, pastor, prophet, or whoever tells you, if it contradicts what you *know* for a fact God has already revealed to you, don't accept or act on it! Wait for *His* confirmation to you.

I've heard many Christians say, "God would never send a message to someone else to give to you." I believe that to be true only if you know His voice distinctly from all others, such as your own thoughts and/or thoughts the enemy may put into your head. If you can't distinctly recognize His voice as His sheep ought to, or if you're ignoring what He's trying to show you out of fear or whatever it may be, I've noticed that the Lord will often go to extreme measures to forewarn you or open your eyes, and sometimes He uses other people to do so (1 Samuel 3, 2 Samuel 12).

***

When the Lord has placed an anointing on your life, you must guard and protect it, along with your joy, peace, temperament and self-control.

There was a time when I would literally feel Satan pulling something out of my spirit. It was the sensation of my spirit lifting up out of my chest. It would come out of nowhere—all of a sudden I'd feel something being pulled out of my chest (spirit). I think it was my joy, because immediately after, I'd develop an unsettling depression.

I would beat myself up over it because I wouldn't react. I'd just stand there like, for lack of better words, a punk—allowing the enemy to steal something away from me that wasn't his without even fighting back. I just felt helpless. But as time went on, and I developed a closer relationship with the Lord, I began to gain knowledge of how much power I had over my life (through God) and against Satan.

✳ So the next time he tried the same old trick, I fought back in Jesus' name! When I felt that joy or whatever starting to pull away from my spirit and out of my chest, I'd rip it right back down, square out of his hands! Remember, what God has for you, is for *you*. Fight for it with the full armor of God:

"Finally, my brethren, be strong in the Lord and in the power of His might. Put on the whole armor of God, that you may be able to stand against the wiles of the devil. For we do not wrestle against flesh and blood, but against principalities, against powers, against the rulers of the darkness of this age, against spiritual hosts of wickedness in the heavenly places. Therefore take up the whole armor of God, that you may be able to withstand in the evil day, and having done all, to stand. Stand therefore, having girded your waist with truth, having put on the breastplate of righteousness, and having shod your feet with the preparation of the gospel of peace; above all, taking the shield of faith with which you will be able to quench all the fiery darts of the wicked one. And take the helmet of salvation, and the sword of the Spirit, which is the word of God; praying always with all prayer and supplication in the Spirit, being watchful to this end with all perseverance and supplication for all the saints."

- Ephesians 6:10-18

I can't stress this enough: Keep your <u>connection</u> and <u>communication with the Lord.</u> Walk in His ways and go the direction *He* tells you to and you won't be led astray. <u>Refrain from bad company</u> (1 Corinthians 15:33), filter what you allow your eyes to see, what substances you put into your body and be very careful about what type of music you listen to. Without refraining from these things, you could be *inviting* the enemy into your life and on your turf. Ask the Lord for discernment and He will grant it to you.

There are so many things in our everyday life that the enemy tries using to sneak his way *into* our life and harm our anointing. <u>If you start to give in and backtrack</u> <u>(backslide), you could very well lose your anointing for a</u> <u>period of time or forever.</u> It happened in the Bible to <u>King</u> <u>Saul</u> (1 Samuel 15:26-28) and <u>Samson</u> (Judges 16:20), and it still happens today. If you feel like you have lost your anointing or just want to go to a deeper level in Him, the Word of God says to "stir up the gift of God" (2 Timothy 1:6). By doing so, the Lord may grant your anointing back to you.

How do you stir up the gift of God? By continual prayer and worship. Both go hand in hand. When you pray, pray for others more than yourself and He will restore you (Job 42:10). When you worship Him, *worship* Him! Gush over Him. Praise Him for Who He *is.* This way you'll grow closer to Him and He will allow things to become available to you that otherwise would not have been.

I love worship and the results of worship. When I do, miracles happen and I learn His heart!

Also, if you go into Theology studies or seminary, please, please, please keep that steady relationship open with the Lord. I can't help but notice that many people who come out of these studies end up forming a new perspective of God, putting Him in a box and develop all head knowledge while losing the heart of God. It sincerely breaks my heart when I see people who were once on fire for the Lord go into seminary or a school of theology and come out doubtful of God's supernatural wonders. Supernatural is *Who* God is. Their faith nearly vanishes when they start believing in a "textbook" god.

The God of the Bible is still the God of today, the miraculous power that the first church had in the Book of Acts is still active now. So please, gain the knowledge of the Bible, but more so, keep and sustain the wisdom of the Lord and remain extremely close to Him. You will gain the knowledge while keeping the faith that moves mountains!

Keep and sustain the wisdom of God and remain close to Him.

On a side note, don't get wrapped up in titles. They don't define you. A title can be taken away just as quickly as it was given. At the end of the day you will still be *you!*

The Dream of Loss

Justus K.
Bungoma, Kenya

Dreams come to men as designed by God Himself to warn and restrained them from pride and destruction (Job 33:14 -17).

I never valued dreams and visions until it happened to me for real. I had just resigned from my job to take up the work of ministry and full time preaching of the gospel. I bought a small pickup truck and saved some money to start up the business while I was going into the ministry. I shared the vision for my business with my brother who gave me very good advice. He suggested I sell the truck and add the money to what I already had, and then buy a van for transport. It was a very good idea. I was impressed immediately.

In one month, I put together all the money, totaling to 850,000 shillings (almost equivalent to 10,000 US dollars). This is a lot of money in our country, which has a higher poverty index.

The money wasn't enough and I had to find a company that would be willing to take this as a deposit and give me a van. So I went from our home towards Bungoma to Nairobi, by which I found one company named Unique Credit Systems. They accepted my offer and we discussed their terms and conditions. I traveled back home to get the money I had saved up.

On October 2, 2002, I took an evening bus to Nairobi to acquire my assets. I was armed with the money because it was night. As I traveled, I fell asleep on the bus and soon started to dream. I dreamt that I jumped into a very deep valley and tried all that I could in vain to get out. I tried shouting but no one came to my rescue. I cried and cried but none offered me help.

When I awoke from the dream, I was very much terrified. I thought about the dream but couldn't figure out what it meant. As we continued to travel, I fell asleep again, and again I dreamt of traveling. In the dream, I travelled a very long journey and got lost, finding myself in a place surrounded by thorns and bricks. I couldn't move because danger was all around me. So I tried to shout for help. When I looked up, I saw a helicopter hovering over me. It was hovering as if it was inspecting the plantation of the thorns. The people in the helicopter only waved at me and moved on. I was left alone to cry…which I did, until no strength was left inside of me.

Finally, I woke up again, but this time, I was even more disturbed. At this point, I was so worried and also confused as to what all of this meant.

When we finally reached Nairobi, it was still dark. No one was allowed to go out because of security purposes. I dozed off *again* on my chair as I waited for morning to break. A third dream came to me: I was climbing a very high, steep mountain. It was very high to climb, but on top of it I could see people dancing. I was so motivated by the dancing that I pressed very hard to reach the top. When I was almost at the top, I grew extremely tired and was only able to crawl on my knees. The wind was very heavy and it started blowing from the top of mountain towards me. I tried to hold firmly onto the ground but had no strength to resist it, so it blew me like a polythene bag down to the foot of the mountain. Reaching the bottom, I started crying again with much pain in my body. Again, I woke up from my dream.

When I woke up, I contemplated on the three dreams I had but could not link them with what I was doing.

I went to the company office where I was going to get my van and paid all that was demanded; my van was taken for inspection while I waited in the office. During the process of it all, the men who worked there came in and handed me the sticker to my van. I was told the inspectors were busy and that they would take a long time.

Evening came and I was told my vehicle would have to stay in line until the next day to be inspected. So I looked for a hotel to sleep for the night.

Morning arrived and I was to go on waiting.

I didn't realize it would be a trip where they would steal my money! The game went on and on and on, so I got the police involved, but not much could be done due to the corruption in our police force. I tried presenting my case to every institution for help, but all was in vain up to this day.

Now, I remain a poor preacher, everyday fully relying on God. Had I realized that God was warning me in those three dreams, I would have refrained from giving them all of my money.

I had no mentor to teach and guide me. Therefore, I advise all friends out there to be under a spirit filled mentor; to teach and guide you in all that you do.

"For God may speak in one way, or in another, yet man does not perceive it. In a dream, in a vision of the night, when deep sleep falls upon men, while slumbering on their beds, then He opens the ears of men, and seals their instruction. In order to turn man from his deed, and conceal pride from man."

- Job 33:14-17

11

This Jesus

HAVE YOU EVER WONDERED why so many people wholeheartedly love this Man named Jesus? Have you ever wondered why the most love songs ever written to one single Person has been to Jesus Christ for over 2,000 years? How about the fact that more books have been written about Him than anyone else? Have you stopped to ask yourself why Christians have so much love for Jesus?

Seriously, I can't help *but* be fascinated by the depth of which people sincerely, genuinely love Jesus Christ. Go into an art museum and you won't fail to find something commemorating Him. Google His name and you'll currently find over *195 million* results! That's some serious love right there.

Your walk with Christ is so important that it seriously has to be *your own* walk—not your mothers', your fathers', your grandparents' or spouses'. Your walk and relationship with Him is your *own,* because if or when you lose someone close and dear to you, you must come to the true realization (as I have) that their life on this earth was never between you and them, it was between them and God. They may have shared their life with you, but their earthly existence was a matter between them and the Father, because that's Who they go back to when they pass away—if they knew Him.

I've had people admit to me, "You know, my father or mother is a minister, so I must respect what they believe and believe the same things also."

My response is always "No, you don't!"

✳ They have *their* walk with the heavenly Father and you have *your* own walk with the heavenly Father. It's a personal thing, whether you like it or not. Someone once said to me, "When it comes to your walk with the Lord, your parents' ceiling should be your floor." This means, whatever your parents have taught you in the Lord, hold on to it while escalating higher than *they* did. Walk with the Lord and enjoy the heights He will take you.

You must get to the point where it's just you and Him. Until Jesus has all of you and your love, your love is unbalanced and unevenly dispersed. Once you give Him all of your love, Jesus will then evenly dispense it to where it needs to be in perfection, therefore making a flawless equation.

Spend time in prayer with Him. If you don't know how to pray, Jesus tells you how to in Matthew 6:9-13. Read it. I've had people tell me that I should pray to so-and-so for help with certain situations, but here's a strict rule that I live by: I *only* pray to God! I don't pray to dead people. **I pray to the One Whom the grave couldn't hold!**

Believe me, knowing Jesus and letting Him into my life was the single best thing I have ever done, because now He lives inside of me. God *resides* in me. Everything I have written in this book is true, and the God Whom I gush about in this book is Truth Himself (John 14:6).

If you want to get to know Jesus Christ personally, the One Whom the grave couldn't hold, you can get to know Him right now. Simply pray this prayer and mean it from your heart:

"Dear Jesus, I am a sinner. I believe that You are God and that you died on the cross for me to take away my sins. I believe that You arose from the dead on the third day and are preparing a place for me in Heaven right now. I repent. Please forgive me for all of my sins. Come into my heart and live inside of me forever. In Jesus' name, Amen."

If you prayed that prayer, you became a child of God and are now born again. Congratulations!

✳ The Bible says that Heaven rejoices when even one soul repents and turns to the Lord (Luke 15:7). To repent means to completely turn away from your sins. Now that you are born again (saved), it is crucial that you get into a Bible-based church (not opinion based), surround yourself with Godly people, talk to God and read the Bible daily.

✳ *"That if you confess with your mouth the Lord Jesus and believe in your heart that God has raised Him from the dead, you will be saved. Nor is there salvation in any other, for there is no other name under Heaven given among men by which we must be saved."*

-Romans 10:9 & Acts 4:12

ACKNOWLEDGEMENTS

FIRST AND FOREMOST, I would like to thank the Lover of My Soul, Jesus Christ, for putting the heavy urge on my spirit to write and complete this book. The days when I felt sluggish, You'd give me the energy to put some "pep in my step". Without You, this book, revealing *more* of Your marvelous works, would have never come to fruition.

I would like to thank my wonderful, amazing and incomparable husband, Edward, for all of the long nights you had to endure me staying up late to finish this book. Thank you from the bottom of my heart for the support and encouragement you've always given me, and all of the days and the nights you prayed *with* me. You're my hero, as well as my best friend. I love you!

I would like to thank my two daughters, Eva and Jewel, for your curiosity, along with all of your questions. You made my heart "pitter-patter" when you would watch me type and say, "Mommy, I wanna write a book just like you." You will, sweethearts. You'll write some even better someday. I believe in you. Just remember to always put

God first above everything/everyone else and follow His lead. He knows the way and will *never* get you lost. Not a day goes by that I'm not proud of you two. Words cannot express how much I love you!

I would like to thank my loving mother, Joyce Johnson, for being my second set of eyes for this book and the long nights you stayed awake to help me out. Not only that, but thanks for all of your motherly help, love and advice. No one could do it better than you. I love you.

I would like to thank my father, Lorenzo Jones, for all of your love, support, encouragement and our long conversations about the Lord. You teach me "a thing or two about a thing or two" with all of your Bible knowledge. And how could I finish this off without thanking you for the fantastic artwork you put towards this book? Thanks, Daddy. I love you.

I would like to thank my sister, Leslie Jones, for all of our debates and for always making me laugh along the way. You're *definitely* one of a kind. Love ya!

Thank you to my in-laws, Bernice and Edward Bagnaschi, for your love.

I would like to thank my editor, Jesse Drake, for all of your hard work and dedication. You're a lifesaver.

ACKNOWLEDGEMENTS

I would like to thank Buddy Baker, Adele Basson, Sara Diaz, Simone Fairchild, Debra Hopkins, Justus Masika Khisa, and Gloria Rivera for allowing me to share your amazing testimonies with the world! Without you, in my heart, this book wouldn't have been complete; therefore, I send you all of my love and appreciation.

I would like to thank my life-long pastor, Pastor Harvill and dear friend, James Walker, Jr. for writing the wonderful reviews that you have for this book. I sincerely appreciate it!

And last, but *certainly* not least, I'd like to thank all of my friends and family for all of your love, support, and for you allowing me to talk your ear off about when I'd finally finish this book. You deserve a medal!

May the Lord Jesus Christ bless every last one of you!

Made in the USA
Monee, IL
26 October 2023